VOYAGE TO MARYLAND (1633)

RELATIO ITINERIS IN MARILANDIAM

VOYAGE TO MARYLAND (1633)

RELATIO ITINERIS IN MARILANDIAM

Original Latin Narrative of Andrew White, S.J.
Translated and Edited by
Barbara Lawatsch Boomgaarden
with Josef IJsewijn

BOLCHAZY-CARDUCCI PUBLISHERS, INC.

• IV •

This Publication Was Made Possible By
PEGASUS LIMITED.

Copyright © 1995 Bolchazy-Carducci Publishers, Inc.
Printed in the United States of America.
Design by Robert Emmet Meagher.
Cover illustration:
Landing of Leonard Calvert and First Maryland Colonists,
oil on canvas by D.A. Woodward,
Maryland Historical Society.

Published by

BOLCHAZY-CARDUCCI PUBLISHERS, INC.

1000 Brown Street, Unit 101
Wauconda, Illinois 60084

LIBRARY OF CONGRESS CATALOGING-IN-PUBLICATION DATA

White, Andrew, 1579-1656
    [Relatio itineris in Marilandiam. English and Latin]
    Voyage to Maryland (1633) = Relatio itineris in Marilandiam /
original Latin narrative of Andrew White, S.J. ; translated and edited by
Barbara Lawatsch-Boomgaarden with Josef IJsewijn.
              p.   cm.
    Includes bibliographical references and index.
    ISBN 0-86516-279-4 (casebound : alk. paper), —
    ISBN 0-86516-280-8 (alk. paper)
    1. Maryland—Description and travel—Early works to 1800.
2. Maryland—History—Colonial period, ca. 1600-1775. 3. Indians of
North America—Maryland—Early works to 1800. 4. Manuscripts, Latin
(Medieval and modern)—Facsimiles. I. Lawatsch-Boomgaarden, Barbara.
II. IJsewijn, J. (Josef). III. Title.
F184.W4916 1995
975.2'02—dc20   95-44434
                                                   CIP

TABLE OF CONTENTS

THE CHARTER
OF
MARY LAND.

 HARLES By the Grace of GOD, King of *England, Scotland, France,* and *Ireland,* Defendor of the Faith, &c. To all to whom thefe Prefents fhall come greeting. WHEREAS Our right Trufty and Wellbeloved Subje& *Cecilius Caluert,* Baron of *Baltemore* in our Kingdom of *Ireland,* Sonne and heire of Sir *George Caluert* Knight, late Ba-

ron

FOREWORD

The early decades of the seventeenth century witnessed the modest beginnings of the settlement of North America by the English. A compelling motive that drove many to risk the perilous sea voyage across the Atlantic and the rigors of existence in the New World was the religious turbulence in Britain. Legal restrictions and persecution of recusants, such as Puritans, Jansenists, and Roman Catholics, caused groups of them to seek havens in America. Those who had a formal education brought with them in their intellectual baggage the memory of Queen Elizabeth, Shakespeare, Ben Jonson, King James I, and Latin, the international language of communication and scholarship, of the Catholic Church, diplomacy, medicine, law.

The Spanish encounter with the New World was a vastly different order. In South America and the Caribbean the conquistadors and the Spanish crown throughout the sixteenth century imposed a religious, cultural and political order that was more Europe-based and uniform than North America exceptionalism, diversity, and localism. Missionary work, religious instruction, and liberal education were introduced and administered by the Roman Catholic orders: Dominicans, Jesuits, Franciscans, Augustinians. They established schools, seminaries and colleges, and introduced the traditional curriculum of the mother country with the study of the Latin language as basic. In the mother country there flowered the *Siglo de Oro* (Golden Age) of Spanish literature. Under the influence of Spanish learning there developed in Latin America the study of comparative ethnography and the view of anthropolitcal humanism, promoted by the religious orders. There emerged a considerable body of significant literature, including the works of Nebrija, Las Casas, José de Acosta, and half-caste Garcilaso de la Vega *"el Inca."* Among the many achievements of the sixteenth century in Latin America were a grammar and dictionary of the native language Nahuatl, an Aztec version of Aesop's fables, and a large volume of Neo-Latin prose and poetry. Before the end of the century there were composed (in Europe) two Neo-Latin epic poems on Columbus's voyage to the New World, by Lorenzo Gambara (1581) and by Giulio Cesare Stella (1585).

The English settlers did not come as conquerors, nor were they motivated by macro-political designs, nor by the quest for gold, views of the "Noble Savage" and a utopian golden age. Their vision was more mundane: economic opportunity and religious freedom. If classical images attracted them, they were such ancient experiences as the voyage of the Argonauts, the wanderings of Aeneas and the Trojans in search of a new home, and Ovid's poetry of exile. An early experience in the Virginia colony was the achievement of George Sandys, a gifted poet who for a decade was on the governor's council as treasury official, and who found the time to compose a verse translation of Ovid's *Metamorphoses* (published 1632) which has been called the "the morning star of poetry and scholarship in the New World," and it has remained one of the classics of English literature. Before coming to Virginia Sandys had written a prose account of a trip through Europe and the Near East entitled *Relation of a Journey* (1615).

Father White's narrative of his part in, and reaction to, the settlement of Maryland finds its place among the reactions of other pioneers in North America, such as those by William Strachey, "A True Repertory of the Wreck and Redemption of Sir Thomas Gates ... His Coming to Virginia and the Estate of that Colony" (1610; published 1625); Alexander Whitaker, "Good News from Virginia" (1613); John Smith, "A True Relation of Such Occurrences and Accidents of Noate as Hath Happened in Virginia Since the First Planting of the Colony" (1608); John Rolfe, "Relation of the State of Virginia Lefte by Sir Thomas Dale Knight in May Last 1616"; John Cotton, "God's Promise to His Plantations" (1630); John Winthrop, "A Model of Christian Charity" (1630); William Morell, "New Anglia" (1623-25, Latin verse with English translation); Thomas Martin, "The New English Canada" (1637); William Bradford "Of Plymouth Plantation" (1630-1651); Samuel Danforth composed almanac verses (c. 1647).

In New England the Puritans who settled in the Bay Colony soon succeeded in naturalizing in American soil the traditional classical curriculum of the mother country with the central elements of Latin language, Roman literature, Roman antiquities and a smattering of Greek. The birthplace of classical learning in North America was the Boston Latin School, founded in 1635, followed by the establishment of Harvard College in 1636. From these beginnings emerged the numerous grammar schools and academies of North America, the other colonial colleges, and a considerable body of Latin prose and of Neo-Latin poetry. We are indebted to Professor Leo Kaiser for his pioneering studies of these works. Easily accessible is his *Early American Latin Verse (1625-1825): An Anthology of American Neo-Latin Poetry* (Chicago: Bolchazy-Carducci, 1985).

It was in this peculiarly North American English pioneering settlements that Father Andrew White (S. J.) came to Maryland (*terra Maria*). He was over fifty years of age when the vessel that brought him from England sailed into Chesapeake Bay. After a long career training for the Jesuit Order on the continent and teaching at various Jesuit colleges, "the apostle of Maryland," as he has been called, furtively embarked on the long, hazardous transatlantic journey to join the proprietary colony of Lord Baltimore to undertake the role of missionary to the Indian tribes of the area as well as non-Catholic settlers of the colony. Father White while in England had written *Decelaratio Coloniae Domini Baronis de Baltimore*. At the new settlement he celebrated a mass and participated in what came to be known as "Maryland Day," the ceremonial birthday of the colony, on Annunciation Day in 1634. Father White had little secular interest in the peopling and conduct of the colony. In ten years his missionary zeal among the various neighboring Indian tribes won him some successes. His greatest accomplishment as missionary was the conversion of the chieftain of the Pisctaway Indians and his wife. His training as a linguist enabled him to compose a grammar and dictionary of the dominant Algonquin language, as well as a catechism, the first philological work of scholarship in North America. His work was cut short by a Puritan insurrection in 1645, when he was brought back in irons to England.

Father White's account of his "Journey to Maryland," sent to Jesuit headquarters in Rome is one of the earliest Neo-Latin works composed in North America. Its literary style, while conventional, exhibits Father White's skill in classical rhetorical usages adapted to contemporary events and issues. Dr. Barbara Lawatsch-Boomgarden has given us both an updated edition of the text together with guidelines for reading and profiting from this pioneering work of one of the first Jesuits in North America and his zeal in propagating their faith.

Meyer Reinhold
Professor of Classical Studies, Boston University
Co-President, International Society for the Classical Tradition

PREFACE

There has been no edition of the Latin version of Andrew White's *Relatio* available to the general reader for almost a century, an astonishing fact when one considers the historical significance and literary merits of his eye-witness account. All previous printings (the most recent ones being that of Thomas Hughes and the edition by E.A. Dalrymple based on W. McSherry's handwritten copy) go back to the only known manuscript, a seventeenth-century office copy kept at the Archives of the Society of Jesus in Rome.[1] When I first compared the Hughes and Dalrymple editions I was struck by the many differences between them, including occasional variations which seemed incongruous considering the high quality of White's prose. By examining the Roman manuscript I have been able to solve the problems created by these discrepancies and to prepare the first critical edition of the text. An extensive introduction with selected bibliography, running vocabulary and notes, a translation of the Latin text, a photographic reproduction of the manuscript and several maps and illustrations have also been provided.

I am deeply grateful to Fathers Rudolf Kutschera, S.J., Vienna, Austria, Richard Plaickner, S.J., Rome, and László Szilas, S.J., of the Archivum Historicum Societatis Iesu, Rome, whose efforts enabled me to use the seventeenth century office copy of Father White's *Relatio* for this edition. My special thanks go to Father W. Gramatowski, S.J., Archivist of the Archivum Romanum Societatis Iesu, who made my work at the ARSI a positive experience in every respect, to Jozef IJsewijn of the Catholic University of Louvain, who generously agreed to collaborate on the edition, to Meyer Reinhold of Boston University, who was kind enough to write a preface, and to Michel V. Ronnick of the Wayne State University and John D. Krugler of Marquette University, whose expertise was of tremendous help to me in improving the edition in a number of ways. I am particularly grateful to Fritz Fellner and Wolfgang Speyer of the University of Salzburg for their lucid comments and unwavering support. To Father R.E. Curran, S.J., of Georgetown University, Wayne Clarke of the Jefferson-Patterson Museum, Maryland, Lois G. Carr and Henry Miller of Historic St. Mary's City, Edward C. Papenfuse of the Maryland State Archives, Russell R. Menard of the University of Minnesota, Alexander MacGregor of the University of Illinois at Chicago, and Lisa Staley, Salzburg/University of Portland, I express my appreciation for valuable suggestions. Special thanks are due to Raimund Kerbl, Gerhard Petersmann, and Walter Steinbichler, University of Salzburg, for their support of the

---

1 Andrew White, "Relatio itineris in Marilandiam," ed. E.A. Dalrymple, in *Fund Publication No.7* (Baltimore: Maryland Historical Society, 1874), pp. 10-43; Thomas Hughes, *History of the Society of Jesus in North America, Documents,* Vol. 1 (Cleveland: The Burrows Brothers Company, 1908), pp. 94-107.

project, and to Thomas Habersatter, Gerald Fliegel, and Josef Falzberger, Salzburg, and Thomas Burg, Vienna/Minneapolis, whose computer expertise and patience were indispensible for the completion of this edition. I would also like to thank John Sarkissian of Youngstown State University and Sister J. Billow, S.N.D., of the Notre Dame Provincial Center, Toledo, Ohio, whose interest in the edition has been an inspiration to me. The staffs of many institutions have provided assistance to me, notably those of the Division of Arts and Letters and the Library of St. Mary's College of Maryland, the Lauinger Library of Georgetown University, the Maryland Historical Society, the Maryland State Archives, the University Library of Salzburg, Austria, the University Library of Graz, Austria, the New York City Public Library, and the Map Room at Harvard University. I am especially grateful to Bolchazy-Carducci Publishers and their staff, particularly Georgine Cooper, for their efforts on behalf of this edition. I also want to thank my brother Peter, his family, and the Spier family for their contributions to this book. To my husband Don I dedicate my affectionate gratitude for his help and support, without which this book would not have been possible.

INTRODUCTION

When the *Ark* and *Dove* weighed anchor in the fall of 1633, most members of the Maryland expedition were doubtlessly motivated by a desire to better their economic and social situation in the New World, as were many other British adventurers and colonists at the time. A good part of the prospective Maryland settlers sought to escape religious persecution, a goal shared with the early colonists of New England. Yet, the expedition did have characteristics which made it different from all others that regularly departed from the British Isles throughout the seventeenth century. Not the least of these was the ultimate purpose of the endeavor, to found the first colony designed as a safe haven for English Catholics in English speaking North America. This goal brought together two powerful forces: the Calverts, one of the most enterprising, capable families of the English aristocracy, and the Society of Jesus, arguably the most successful missionaries of the baroque period.

George Calvert (?1580-1632), the initiator of the expedition, had risen from obscure origins to occupy important positions in the civil service by dint of hard work and administrative competence.[1] At the age of thirty he was selected as clerk of the Privy Council, and in 1619 James I (1603-1625) appointed him a secretary of state. When Calvert left this office in 1625, the king recognized his accomplishments by elevating him to the Irish peerage as Baron of Baltimore. Around the same time Calvert decided to openly embrace Roman Catholicism, the faith that his father abandoned under legal pressure during George's youth. The ever shifting political climate coupled with his avowed Catholicism made it difficult for Calvert to return to public office. After a sojourn in Ireland, he devoted his energies to developing a Catholic colony on the snowswept Avalon peninsula in Newfoundland, which he briefly visited in the summer of 1627. He moved there with his family in 1628, but the harsh climate , the hostile French in neighboring settlements, and the outbreak of disease forced him to abandon plans to settle permanently. Before leaving, he sought to obtain the king's approval for a grant for a colony further south, in the northern Chesapeake area.

To satisfy the religious needs of his Catholic subjects, Baltimore engaged the services of two members of the Society of Jesus. While in Avalon he apparently corresponded with another Jesuit who would do much to make the Maryland colony a success, Andrew White, S.J. (1579-1656).[2] When White received permission to participate in the Calverts' second expedition and to lay the foundations of a Jesuit mission in Maryland, he had a proven record of accomplishment. Born to an English family, possibly in London, White matriculated at Douai College in 1593 and subsequently studied philosophy and theology at several colleges primarily in Spain. Ignoring the so-called penal laws, particularly the statute of 1585, which made it an act of treason for a Catholic priest to enter or remain in England, White returned home after his ordination in 1605. His return coincided with the Gunpowder Plot, a supposed conspiracy against the King and Parliament involving a handful of Catholics. Although there is no evidence that White was connected with it, he left England with a number of priests, many of whom were banished on pain of death. Shortly afterwards White was accepted into the Jesuit novitiate at Louvain. Eventually White taught theology, scripture, and Hebrew at the Jesuit Colleges at Louvain and Liège. He also returned to England on several missions, despite the constant threat of arrest and execution. Although as prefect of studies at Liège he enjoyed a reputation as a scholar and a position of some authority, his theological views, which included a strict adherence to the doctrines of Thomas Aquinas (1225-1274), created problems for him in his order, and by 1630 he no longer held his position in Liège. One suspects that White's daring and impetuous personality did not serve him well in the halls of academe.

The Jesuits seemed not to wish White's abilities to go wasted, however, and found other projects more fit for his adventurous nature. Although the Newfoundland colony failed to achieve their goals, the Calverts were not prepared to forsake their dream for a colony in America. White had a major role in achieving that vision. The Avalon patent became the model for the charter of a new colony, Maryland, which was named after the (Catholic) Queen of Charles I, Henrietta Maria. When George died in April 1632, his eldest son Cecilius, at age 26, used his father's political connections to procure the final grant in June of the same year, despite fierce opposition from representatives of the Virginia colony.[3] The continuing political threats to the Maryland Charter prevented Cecilius Calvert from leaving England and living in Maryland. His capable administration provided the basis for the success of the colony. Partially to placate his opponents in London and the Virginians in the New World, and above all in order to attract enough investors and prevent disruption of civil order among colonists, Cecilius promised separation of church and state and guaranteed the rights to vote and hold office to all free man in the Maryland colony, regardless of religion.

Cecilius appointed his younger brother Leonard the leader of the expedition and first governor of Maryland, and instructed him particularly with regard to maintaining harmony among members of different denominations. The *Relatio* reveals that, although there were some tensions between Protestant and Catholic members of the expedition, no major incidents occurred. Leonard Calvert was also successful, for the most part, in his negotiations with various colonial dignitaries and native rulers whose cooperation he needed during the voyage and the establishment of the first settlement. Due to his brother's foresight and some favorable circumstances, the expedition obtained supplies in Virginia, even though the Virginia settlers were understandably opposed to the new colony, since it effectively destroyed the economic and religious hegemony they enjoyed in the Chesapeake region. That the mollification of the Virginians was of utmost importance to the Calverts and their Jesuit advisors is made clear by the advantages the Marylanders eventually enjoyed, particularly in form of the assistance rendered by Protestants like Henry Fleet, a fur trader who had lived among the Chesapeake Indians for years.

The concern for such practical matters is evident in the pages of the *Relatio*, which contains valuable information about the daily lives of the colonists. Even so, the *Relatio* is also a spiritual document. In this sense it resembles the many other 'relations' of the period, reports submitted by all Jesuit houses and missions to keep their superiors informed. White's *Relatio* was sent to the Father General of the Jesuits at the time, Mutius Vitelleschi, in Rome. An English report (up until now the primary source of information on the first voyage) also ascribed to White was sent to a business partner of the Calverts. While the two documents are similar and for the most part based on the same information, they are not identical. The Latin version reveals much more about White's character, aspirations, and interests, and is of much higher literary quality. It also draws a more vivid picture of the object of the Jesuit's missionary zeal, the Algonquian tribes of the Chesapeake region.

Given the essentially prosaic nature of the *Relatio*, and the limitations of time and resources on White, one is struck by its stylistic refinement. Though there are some deviations from classical standards (see note on the text and running notes), the *Relatio* is written in a sophisticated, often elegant humanist idiom. The narrative abounds in periodic, though not overly convoluted sentences, with the subordinate clause preceding or surrounding the main clause and additional subordinate clauses, *ablativi absoluti*, and *participia coniuncta*, which bring further variety to the text. One can find particularly elegant formulations involving hyperbata, other figures of word order and even occasional rhythmic *clausulae*, as in *utebamur peritissimo*. Figures such as hyperbaton lend a particular emphasis to the narration, by drawing attention either to positive circumstances and qualities, or to the power of nature, such as the fierceness of a rainstorm (*atrocem impluit imbrem*), the threatening aspects of clouds before a storm (*glaucas cogente nubes vento gravidas*), the ability and experience of the captain (*navarcho utebamur peritissimo*), and the friendly and sociable attitude of the Yaocomico Indians (*nostro gaudent uti consortio*).

White's delight in the beauty and bounty of nature is reflected in his extensive descriptions. Though he was clearly interested in the practical application of natural resources and in conveying substantive botanical (or otherwise scientifically useful) information, some of his phrases have a decidedly poetic flair, as when he refers to cotton harvested on Barbados as *nive candidius et pluma mollius*. He enhances his enthusiastic description of the pineapple by praising its color in a phrase resounding with assonance and alliteration: *coloris aurei virore mixta gratissima*. When trying to explain items and facts utterly foreign to his readers, White frequently uses antitheses to clarify his point. The figure is effectively employed, for instance, to describe the "cabbage tree" (*arboris magnae truncum adaequans, neque tamen arbor sed legumen*) and to convey a sense of the impression which the Potomac River made on its early European visitors (*nullis inficitur paludibus, sed solida utrinque terra assurgent decentes arborum silvae, neque clausae vepretis*). White also uses antitheses to emphasize a point central to his description of the Yaocomico Indians of Maryland when pointing to the reasonable nature of their decision-making process (*nil decernunt...subito arrepti motu animi, sed ratione*) and when presenting face-painting as an understandable choice of comfort over appearance (*commodo suo magis intenti quam decori*). As has been pointed out by Eduard Norden in *Antike Kunstprosa*, the use of antithesis represents a prime example of the influence of ancient rhetoric, specifically the work of Isocrates and Cicero, on the styles of Renaissance authors, especially in England. However, while some writers were affecting an antithetical style primarily for the sake of imitating the styles of ancient models, White's antitheses in the descriptions of the *Relatio* serve a practical purpose as well, namely to stress important messages contained in his account and to convey a more distinct impression of peoples, items and places completely unknown to his readers in the Old World.

Despite White's frequent references to flora and fauna, the Jesuit's main interest was directed towards Native Americans. By 1634 the Society of Jesus, whose missionary outposts could be found in all four corners of the globe, was well aware of the problems arising from diverse cultural attitudes, and its members commented in their extensive writings on the necessity to adapt their approach to each culture. One may assume, as the Calverts probably did, that the Jesuits in Lord Baltimore's expedition were familiar with these issues. White's interest and missionary intent are obvious in the astonishing amount and detail of information he conveys about the Maryland chiefdoms, as well as in the positive tone of his descriptions. That his initial enthusiasm and missionary fervor were matched by his endurance and ability is illustrated by his activities and effectiveness as recorded in the Jesuits' yearly reports and especially by the fact that he learned to speak the local Algonquian language better than any other Jesuit in the early years — and probably better than most settlers; fragments of a catechism in the Piscataway language ascribed to him can still be viewed at Georgetown University.[4]

Perhaps the best way of evaluating White's account of the Native Americans is by comparing it with other primary sources and what we now know about the situation when the first Europeans arrived. The people of the Maryland chiefdoms White refers to (Piscataway, Yaocomico, Patuxent) as well as the Patawomecks on the Virginia side of the Potomac, were all Algonquian-speakers, that is, they belonged to the Algonquian language family, which was dominant along most of the eastern seaboard of North America at the time of the establishment of European colonies. The Maryland Algonquians as well as the Patawomecks were, however, under attack by the Iroquois-speaking Susquehannocks, also mentioned by White, and by other Iroquois-speakers. Several chiefdoms of Maryland formed a loose alliance under the leadership of the Piscataways, whose chieftain, called *imperator* in the *Relatio*, was the paramount chief, or *tayac*, of this confederation.[5]

The Patawomecks, whose chieftain was first visited by Governor Calvert and, according to the *Relatio*, exhibited great openness towards the English leader and the missionary in his company, were apparently members of the Piscataway confederation. Their chief took pains to retain his independence from the Piscataways as well as from the expanding Powhatan hegemony of Virginia, even though his chiefdom was under constant pressure from periodic raids of the Iroquois. This situation explains why the Patawomecks saw the Maryland settlers as potential allies and received them in an especially friendly manner. The *Relatio* comments only briefly on Governor Calvert's next visit to the paramount chief, called *emperor* by White, of the Piscataways, though the Jesuit does convey a sense of the importance of this encounter. The Piscataways were to form the most natural and stable alliance with Lord Baltimore's colony.

While cultural ties and social relations were strong between the Maryland and the Virginia Algonquians, there was also a certain amount of rivalry between the Powhatans of Virginia and the Piscataways of Maryland. More importantly, William Claiborne, a fur trader from Virginia mentioned in the *Relatio* as an enemy to the Maryland colony, was trading intensively and had formed a military alliance with the Susquehannocks, the Piscataways' most threatening enemies.[6] Claiborne, who had established a trading post on Kent Island within the area granted to Lord Baltimore, refused to give up his trade monopoly or acknowledge the sovereignty of the Calverts and rallied the Susquehannocks to his side. Not surprisingly the paramount chief, or *tayac* of the Piscataways, Kittamaquund, (who faced additional challenges due to his usurpation of power from his brother), was as anxious to form close ties with the Maryland colony as was Governor Calvert to cooperate with the Piscataways. This alliance was strengthened when Kittamaquund graciously received White and converted to Catholicism with his family and a number of other Piscataways in 1641.

The settlers' immediate concerns centered on the Yaocomico Indians, whose lifestyle White describes extensively. Their village was located along the St. Mary's River (called St. George's River in the *Relatio*) in Southern Maryland. Following Henry Fleet's advice, the English settlers sailed there from St. Clement's Island and found the Yaocomicos already preparing to move away under the pressure of Susquehannock attacks. Although the *Relatio* seems to suggest that the Yaocomicos were part of the Piscataway hegemony, other evidence indicates that they were autonomous.[7] Nonetheless, the Yaocomicos shared much in common with the Piscataways and other Algonquians of Maryland, and White's description of their life style is one of the few known to exist. Their society was hierarchical and reserved a number of privileges for a small aristocracy, who are referred to as *principes viri* in the *Relatio* and included the chief, councillors, war captains, and probably members of a priestly class. Among the status symbols of the tidewater Algonquians were the copper ornaments observed by White in the possession of some Yaocomicos.

Comparisons with the more plentiful sources on the Powhatans of Virginia show some significant similarities between the cultures described, concerning, for instance, dress, hairstyle, food, and dwellings.[8] The so-called longhouse, for instance, described in detail by White, can be found on engravings based on the watercolors of John White (no relation), who was depicting scenes on the Virginian side of the Potomac. Similarly, the "frenzied spirit" called "Ochre" in White's account obviously corresponds with a deity variously called "Oke", "Okee", "Okeus", etc. in Virginian sources, and the distinction between him and a "good god" who did not have to be worshipped or appeased in any way emerges from other reports as well. Since ceremonials were rarely witnessed or described by seventeenth century Englishmen, White's description of a ceremonial of the Patuxent is particularly interesting, even though the Jesuit was not an eyewitness. The Patuxent were part of a small alliance of chiefdoms on the lower western shore of Maryland, and their chieftain, towards whom White first turned his missionary efforts, presented the Jesuit Fathers with a valuable piece of cultivated land during the beginning years of their mission.

In addition to their mission among the Indians, however, the Jesuits also tended to the spiritual and practical needs of the English settlers. White correctly assumed that the colony would not suffer from lack of food: deer, fish, and fowl were abundant. The soil produced sufficient corn and vegetables, but it turned out to be especially favorable to raising tobacco, which became the main source of income for the settlers, and remains an important crop in Maryland to this day. Although the returns of agriculture were not as high as those that the Calverts had hoped to obtain in the fur trade, which had been expected to provide the colony's economic base, tobacco was still quite profitable. Since tobacco growing is labor intensive and labor was scarce, wages in the colony were high, allowing for considerable upward mobility. While a number of early colonists had come as indentured servants (there were no slaves in early Maryland), the vast majority of those who survived became independent landowners themselves during the first decades of the colony.

The main impediment to such advancement was disease, especially malaria and dysentery, which carried off approximately one-fifth of the newly arrived settlers and a number of Jesuits during the first eight years.[9] White himself had to return to St. Mary's City periodically to recover from illnesses. Despite his advanced age, however, he seems to have adapted better than many others, since he survived a longer stay in Maryland than most other missionaries in the first decade. His strong constitution and positive outlook were undoubtedly of great use to him during these hard times.

Hostilities, mostly with other Englishmen in the area and with the Susquehannock allies of William Claiborne, also took their toll on the Maryland settlers. Claiborne remained their nemesis for many years, as White sensed already when he wrote the *Relatio*. Within the colony itself, relations between Lord Baltimore and the Jesuits were not always harmonious, either. A dispute arose only a few years after the first expedition over the Jesuits' acquisition of land throught the gift of the Patuxent chieftain.[10] While this controversy was eventually settled through negotiation, challenges from the outside brought violence and devastation to Maryland. Great damage was done to the Maryland colony when White's mission was drastically cut short during the chaotic time of civil war. In 1645 Captain Richard Ingle, a shipmaster with ties to the increasingly Puritan-dominated English Parliament, having obtained supportive letters from members of Parliament, invaded Maryland with his crew in order to seize or destroy all Catholic property. He took the colony's leaders and two Jesuits, including White, as prisoners to England. Governor Leonard Calvert was able to escape to Virginia and returned to Maryland to restore order in late 1646.

White was not so fortunate. As it was illegal for a Catholic priest to set foot on English soil, White and the other Jesuit were immediately thrown into prison on arrival in England, and remained there for three years. When the trial was finally held, the Jesuit Fathers defended themselves on the grounds that they had been brought to England by force. This argument prevailed, and the Jesuits were banished. White's petition to his superiors for permission to return to Maryland was (mercifully) rejected. The fact that, at almost seventy years of age, he was still willing to undergo the struggles of life in the New World is yet another tribute to his impetuous nature. He did manage, with characteristic disdain for civil authority, to return to England, where he died in 1656.

The Jesuit presence in Maryland, however, did not end with White's departure. While the interests of the Calverts, the proprietors of Maryland, and the Jesuits diverged in certain areas even in the early years of the colony, the connection between them remained strong. The Patuxent's gift of land in particular became an object of dispute. Yet the Jesuits' presence contributed much to the friendly relations between the settlers and most adjoining chiefdoms. Moreover, the Society of Jesus was among the chief investors in the early years of the colony, and thus played a vital role in the realization of the Calverts' vision. Conversely, the Jesuits were able to create the foundation for a province in British North America through their cooperation with the Calverts. It is no accident that Maryland served as an important base of operations for the Jesuits in the United States, and that Baltimore became the first archdiocese in the country. Jesuit spirituality has also left its mark on southern Maryland, the site of the settlers' first landing, where the devout Catholicism of its natives is proverbial.

White's *Relatio*, along with the corresponding English version ascribed to him, remains the most vivid and detailed account of the expedition that resulted in the establishment of the Maryland colony. While the perceptiveness of the Jesuit's observations and the elegance of his Latin owes much to his association with the sophisticated intellectual milieu of Louvain, Liège, and other centers of learning on the continent, White's interest in natural science and his remarkably forward-looking approach to natural science seem typically British. Certainly his emphasis on empirical observation and his ridicule of superstition as a basis for knowledge have much in common with other British thinkers such as Francis Bacon, who prepared the way for the scientific methodology of our time. Thus, while we do not know where White received his early education, his contacts with educated Englishmen connected him with the distinguished humanist tradition of England, where schools and universities were carrying on the legacy of outstanding scholars such as Thomas More, Thomas Linacre, and John Colet. White not only enjoyed the advantages of Jesuit training, but also had additional access to the great humanist traditions of Europe. His *Relatio itineris in Marilandiam* stands as a significant document in the classical tradition of the English colonies of North America.

NOTES

1 An overview of George Calvert's life and an analysis of his impact on the Maryland colony is presented in Russell R. Menard and Lois Green Carr, "The Lords Baltimore and the Colonization of Maryland," in David B. Quinn, ed., *Early Maryland in a Wider World* (Detroit, Mich.: Wayne State University Press, 1982), pp. 167-215. For detailed analyses of George Calvert's life and career see: John D. Krugler, "The Face of a Protestant and the Heart of a Papist': A Reexamination of Sir George Calvert's Conversion to Roman Catholicism," *Journal of Church and State* 20 (Autumn, 1978): 507-531, and "The Calvert Family, Catholicism, and Court Politics in Early Seventeenth-Century England," *The Historian* 43 (May, 1981):378-392.

2 There are still many questions yet to be answered concerning the life of White. Although the general outline of his life can be gleaned from a variety of documents, such as a *Necrologium* in the Jesuit Archives in Rome, these sources are sometimes vague, or even contradictory on specific points and dates. Biographic information on White can be found in: Carlos Sommervogel, *Bibliothèque de la Compagnie de Jésus,* vol. 8 (Brussels, 1898), cols. 1091-93; Thomas A. Hughes, *History of the Society of Jesus in North America,* Text, Vol. 1 and Documents, Vol. 1 (Cleveland: Burrows Brothers Company, 1908), and J.A. Leo Lemay, *Men of Letters in Colonial Maryland* (Knoxville: University of Tennessee Press, 1972), with an extensive bibliography.

3 For a discussion of Cecilius Calvert's role in the establishment of the colony and the early years of the colony see: Menard and Carr, "The Lords Baltimore" and John D. Krugler, "Lord Baltimore, Roman Catholics, and Toleration: Religious Policy in Maryland During the Early Catholic Years, 1634-1649," *The Catholic Historical Review* 65 (January, 1979): 49-75. Studies on various aspects of the colonization of Maryland are contained in: Quinn, *Early Maryland.* The standard reference for the early history of Maryland is Robert Brugger's *Maryland: A Middle Temperament, 1634-1980* (John's Hopkins University Press, 1988).

4 The development of the Jesuit missions in southern Maryland is traced in: Edwin W. Beitzell, *The Jesuit Missions of St. Mary's County, Maryland* (Abell, 1959) and Gerald P. Fogarty, "The Origins of the Missions 1634-1776" in *The Maryland Jesuits, 1634-1833* (Baltimore: Maryland Province, 1976):9-27. Important sources and additional information concerning White and the Maryland mission are found in: Robert Emmett Curran, S.J., *American Jesuit Spirituality. The Maryland Tradition, 1634-1900* (New York, Mahwah: Paulist Press, 1988); Clayton C. Hall, *Narratives of Early Maryland, 1633-1684* (New York, 1919; reprint New York: Barnes & Noble 1967); Hughes, *History*, and Henry J. Foley, *Records of the English Province of the Society of Jesus* (London, 1878). For a recent assessment of the Jesuits see: John D. Krugler and Timothy B. Riordan, "'Scandalous and offensive to the Government': The 'Popish Chappel' at St. Mary's City, Maryland, and the Society of Jesus, 1634 to 1705," *Mid-America* 73, 3 (October, 1991): 187-208.

5 For a detailed analysis of alliances, relations and cultural similarities between chiefdoms on the Potomac and the Patuxent see: Wayne E. Clark and Helen C. Rountree, "The Powhatans and the Maryland Mainland," in *Powhatan Foreign Relations. 1500-1722*, ed. by Helen C. Rountree (Charlottesville, London: University of Virginia Press, 1993), pp. 112-135.

6 Stephen R. Potter, *Commoners, Tribute, and Chiefs. The Development of Algonquian Culture in the Potomac Valley* (Charlottesville, London: University of Virginia Press, 1993), pp. 188-193, focuses on Claiborne's alliance with the Susquehannocks, while Aubrey C. Land, *Colonial Maryland. A History* (Millwood, N.Y.: KTO Press, 1989), pp. 6-54, places the controversy within the context of the development of the colony.

7 Clark, p. 116.

8 The most recent and comprehensive study of Powhatan culture is Helen C. Rountree, *The Powhatan Indians of Virginia: Their Traditional Culture* (Norman: University of Oklahoma Press, 1989).

9 Menard and Carr, "The Lords Baltimore," p. 190.

10 For an analysis of this controversy see: John D. Krugler, "Lord Baltimore, Roman Catholics, and Religious Toleration: Religious Policy in Maryland during the Early Catholic Years, 1634-1649," *Catholic Historical Review* 65 (January 1979): 72-73.

NOTE ON THE EDITION

THE MANUSCRIPT

The only seventeenth century manuscript of Andrew White's *Relatio* known to exist today is a contemporary office copy of his letter housed in the Archivum Romanum Societatis Iesu in Rome. The handwriting of the manuscript has been identified by Thomas Hughes as that of a Roman copyist and is not White's, whose hand we know from several autographs among the Stonyhurst College manuscripts. As far as can be determined, however, the copy is faithful to the original. There is much evidence to that effect: the text is stylistically uniform, and the nature of the document makes it rather unlikely that anyone would have altered or added to the original letter. Moreover, the tone of the entire report and the sophistication of content, expression, and style are perfectly compatible with White's biography.

The manuscript comprises pages 413-440 of volume IV, Part I, of *Anglia, Historia*, which is a collection of miscellaneous documents, mostly written by a variety of hands and pertaining to events involving Jesuits in England. As the facsimile shows, the text, written on paper in a modified *Humanistenkursive*, is very well preserved. The document was restored in the twentieth century, probably the 1940s, when the entire volume was rebound and provided with the current page numbers. The leaves on which the *Relatio* is written measure 27 by 20 cm, of which a rectangle of about 22, 5 by 14, 5 cm is covered by writing.

THE PRESENT EDITION

Marginal notes by the same hand summarize or refer to the contents of each paragraph in the manuscript. These notes have been used in the present edition as headlines of the paragraphs to which they relate, while the critical apparatus indicates their approximate position in the text. In the manuscript there are also additional comments, numbers, and lines clearly by a different hand, which has been identified by Thomas Hughes as that of Nathaniel Southwell, the seventeenth century Jesuit historian. These additions explain in part the differences between the previous editions of the *Relatio*, which were prepared more than eighty years ago and have, of course, long been out of print. Dalrymple's edition,[1] which is based on a handwritten copy of the Roman document made by Father W. McSherry in the 19th century and now kept at Georgetown

---

[1] Andrew White, "Relatio itineris in Marilandiam," ed. E.A. Dalrymple, in *Fund Publication No. 7* (Baltimore: Maryland Historical Society, 1874), pp.10-43.

University, incorporates Father Southwell's comments, but omits the marginal notes that are an integral part of the Roman document. They are, however, printed in the margins of Thomas Hughes's edition of the narrative in the *History of the Society of Jesus in North America,* Documents, Vol. 1 (Cleveland: The Burrows Brothers Company, 1908, pp. 94-107), which in turn does not contain Father Southwell's additions. This book presents the first critical edition of the *Relatio* and allows the reader to distinguish between the text itself and various additions by means of the *apparatus criticus* of the edited version as well as through the facsimile section. Running vocabulary and notes, and an English translation have also been provided.

The critical apparatus also notes unusual spellings or mistakes in the manuscript which have been emended in the text. Abbreviations have been expanded, and a few additions that seemed necessary for a clear understanding of the text are supplied in square brackets. Words that appear to be redundant in the manuscript have been enclosed in brackets. The punctuation follows Hughes's edition, or has been modernized by me. Like many Neo-Latin manuscripts, the hand-written version of the *Relatio* in the Jesuit Archives is rather inconsistent with regard to the capitalization of words. The text has therefore been standardized in this respect following other modern editions of Neo-Latin works, particularly the texts printed in Jozef IJsewijn's *Companion to Neo-Latin Studies* (Leuven-Louvain/Atlanta: Leuven University Press/Peeters Press/Scholars Press, 1990).

Despite these conventional adjustments there remain a few features that may be unfamiliar to readers accustomed to classical texts. Deviations from classical standards involve primarily the use of the perfect subjunctive where the sequence of tenses would require the imperfect subjunctive, the use of the indicative in some indirect questions, and, though very rarely, the use of a subjunctive where the indicative would be expected. Irregularities that have not been emended in the text and might cause difficulties are explained in the running vocabulary/notes. I have omitted from the running vocabulary those words contained in Frederic M. Wheelock, *Wheelock's Latin Grammar*, 4th ed. rev. (New York: HarperCollins Publishers, 1992). Words marked with an asterisk in the vocabulary have already appeared three times and will not be glossed again.

BIBLIOGRAPHY

MANUSCRIPT SOURCES

Anglia, Historia, IV. Archivum Romanum Societatis Iesu, Rome.

Anglia, Necrologium, 1578-1732. Archivum Romanum Societatis Iesu, Rome.

The Calvert Papers. Maryland Historical Society, Baltimore, Maryland.

Manuale Sacerdotum. Special Collections Division, Lauinger Library, Georgetown University, Washington, D.C.

Maryland Province Archives, Box 3. Special Collections Division, Lauinger Library, Georgetown University, Washington, D.C

PRINTED SOURCES AND SECONDARY LITERATURE

Beitzell, Edwin W. *The Jesuit Missions of St. Mary's County, Maryland.* Abell, 1959.

Burton, Edwin H. and Thomas L. Williams, eds. *The Douay College Diaries, 1598-1654.* London: Catholic Record Society, 1911.

Brugger, Robert J. *Maryland: A Middle Temperament, 1634-1980.* Baltimore: Johns Hopkins University Press, 1988.

The Calvert Papers. Fund Publications No. 28, 34, and 35. Baltimore: Maryland Historical Society, 1889-99.

Carr, Lois Green. "The Founding of St. Mary's City." *The Smithsonian Journal of History 3* (1968-1969): 77-100.

Chiapelli, Fredi, ed. *First Images of America.* The Impact of the New World on the Old. Vol. 2. Berkeley, Los Angeles, and London: University of California Press, 1976.

Curran. Francis X. "The Mystery of Father White." *Woodstock Letters* 85 (1956): 375-80.

Curran, Robert Emmett. *American Jesuit Spirituality. The Maryland Tradition, 1634-1900.* New York, Mahwah: Paulist Press, 1988.

_____ *The Maryland Jesuits, 1634-1833.* Baltimore: Corporation of the Roman Catholic Clergymen, Maryland Province, Society of Jesus, 1976.

A Declaration of The Lord Baltemore's Plantation in Mary-land (1633). Ed. with introductions by Lois Green Carr, Edward C. Papenfuse, and Lawrence C. Wroth. Annapolis: Maryland Hall of Records Commission, 1983.

Doonan, J.A. "An Historical Sketch of Father Andrew White, S.J., the Apostle of Maryland." *Woodstock Letters 1* (1872): 1-11.

Foley, Henry J. *Records of the English Province of the Society of Jesus.* Vol. 3. London: Burns and Oates, 1878.

Force, Peter, comp. *Tracts and Other Papers Relating Principally to the Origin, Settlement, and Progress of the Colonies in North America, From the Discovery of the Countrey to the Year 1776.* Vol. 4, No. 12. Washington, D.C. , 1846.

Hall, Clayton C. *Narratives of Early Maryland, 1633-1684.* New York, 1919; reprint New York: Barnes & Noble, 1967.

Hughes, Thomas A. *History of the Society of Jesus in North America.* Text, Vol. 1 and Documents, Vol. 1. Cleveland: Burrows Brothers Company, 1908.

Krugler, John D. "The Calvert Family, Catholicism, and Court Politics in Early Seventeenth Century England." *The Historian* 43 (May, 1981):378-392.

_____"'The Face of a Protestant and the Heart of a Papist': A Reexamination of Sir George Calvert's Conversion to Roman Catholicism." *Journal of Church and State* 20 (Autumn, 1978): 507-531.

_____"Lord Baltimore, Roman Catholics, and Toleration: Religious Policy in Maryland During the Early Catholic Years, 1634-1649." *The Catholic Historical Review* 65 (January, 1979): 49-75.

_____ and Timothy B. Riordan, "'Scandalous and offensive to the Government': The 'Popish Chappel' at St. Mary's City, Maryland, and the Society of Jesus, 1634 to 1705." *Mid-America* 73, 3 (October, 1991): 187-208.

Lemay, J.A. Leo. *Men of Letters in Colonial Maryland.* Knoxville: University of Tennessee Press, 1972.

Land, Aubrey, C. *Colonial Maryland. A History.* Millwood, N.Y.: KTO Press, 1989.

Maryland Historical Society. *Fund Publication, No. 7.* Baltimore, 1874.

Potter, Stephen R. *Commoners, Tribute, and Chiefs. The Development of Algonquian Culture in the Potomac Valley.* Charlottesville, London: University of Virginia Press, 1993.

David B. Quinn, ed. *Early Maryland in a Wider World.* Detroit, Mich.: Wayne State University Press, 1982.

A Relation of Maryland together with a map of the Countrey... London, 1635.

Rountree, Helen C., ed. *Powhatan Foreign Relations. 1500-1722.* Charlottesville, London: University of Virginia Press, 1993.

Sommervogel, Carlos. *Bibliothèque de la Compagnie de Jésus.* Vol. 8. Brussels, 1898.

Walsh, Gerald G. "The Spirit of the Maryland Venture, 1634-1644." *Woodstock Letters* 63 (1934): 191-210.

White, Andrew. *A Briefe Relation of the Voyage Unto Maryland.* Annapolis: Maryland Hall of Records, 1984.

Voyage to Maryland

ENGLISH TEXT

NARRATIVE OF A VOYAGE TO MARYLAND

1 • THEY SAIL FROM COWES

On the 22nd of November, 1633, St. Cecilia's Day, with a southeast wind softly blowing, we sailed from Cowes, which is a port on the Isle of Wight. After we had placed the main parts of the ship under the protection of God first, and then of His Most Holy Mother, of St. Ignatius, and of all the angels of Maryland, we sailed for a short time between the two shores. When the wind was failing us, we cast anchor opposite Yarmouth Castle, which is situated toward the northwest of the same island. Here we were received with public cannon salutes; and yet fear was not absent. For the sailors were muttering among themselves that they were expecting a messenger and a letter from London, and for that reason they also seemed to be devising delays. But God destroyed their evil plans. Indeed that very night, when a favorable, but powerful wind was blowing, a French cutter (which had moored in the same port together with us) was forced to sail, and came close to running into our pinnace [i.e., the *Dove*]. Therefore the latter, having cut away and lost one anchor, set sail as fast as possible in order not to be crushed; and since it was a dangerous place to drift, she hurried out to sea. And so, lest we might lose sight of our pinnace, we decided to follow. In this way the plans that the sailors considered against us were foiled. This happened on the 23rd of November, the feast of St. Clement, who obtained the crown of martyrdom when he was tied to an anchor and plunged into the sea, and showed to the people of the earth how they might narrate the wonderful works of God.

2 • THE NEEDLES

On that day, around the tenth morning hour, we were greeted by festive salutes from Hurst Castle. After that we sailed past numerous cliffs situated at the outermost part of the Isle of Wight, which they call the Needles, after their shape. They are feared by seafarers because of the double tide of the sea, that snatches away and dashes ships against the rocks on one side and on the other against the shore, to say nothing of the other danger, however, which we overcame near Yarmouth Castle. For with the wind and surf pushing us, and with our anchor not yet weighed, the ship [i.e, the *Ark*] was almost dashed against the shore, if we had not been suddenly turned away by a great force, and, plunging into the sea, escaped the danger, by the grace of God, who considered us worthy of this pledge of his protection through the merits of St. Clement.

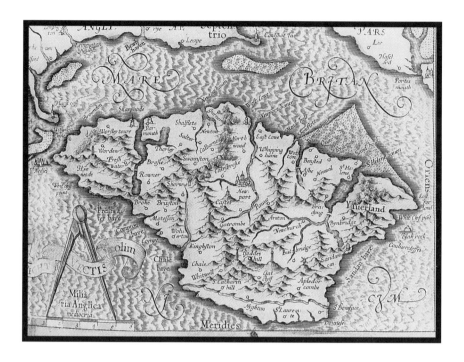

3 • THE SCILLY ISLES

That day, which fell on a Sabbath [i.e., Saturday], and during the following night, we enjoyed such favorable winds that early the next day, around the ninth hour, we left the western promontory of England and the Scilly Isles behind us, and, having turned with a gentle tack more toward the west, we traversed the mouth of the English Channel; but we did not sail as fast as we could have, so that we would not get too far ahead of the pinnace, lest she might become a prey to the Turks and pirates, who were mainly responsible for making that sea dangerous.

Then it happened that a fine merchant ship of six hundred tons, by the name of *Dragon*, caught up with us around three o'clock in the afternoon, bound for Angola after having set out from London. And since there was time now, because we had already overcome the danger, to allow for a little pleasure, it was delightful to see these two ships compete with each other in their journey for an entire hour, to the sound of trumpets, while the sky and the wind were favorable. And our ship would have won, although we did not use the topsail, if we had not been forced to stop because of the pinnace, which was slower. Therefore we yielded to the merchant ship; before evening, however, she sailed past us and passed out of our sight.

4 · TOSSED IN A STORM

Then, on Sunday, the 24th and Monday, the 25th of November we enjoyed fair sailing until evening. At that time, however, the winds turned northerly, and such a storm arose that the London merchant ship, which I mentioned, reversed its course and returned to England and the port at Falmouth. Since our pinnace was a vessel of only forty tons, she, too, began to lose confidence in her strength and, sailing close to us, advised us, that she would indicate, with lights displayed on the masthead, fear of shipwreck. Meanwhile we were sailing in a strong ship of 300 tons [i.e., the *Ark*]—a better one could not be built of wood and iron. We had employed a very experienced captain, who had the option of returning, if he wished, to England, or of further contending with the winds. If he should submit to them, the nearby Irish coast, infamous for its hidden rocks and very frequent shipwrecks, awaited us. The bold spirit of the captain won out nonetheless, as did his desire to test how sturdy the new ship was, which he was handling for the the first time. He decided to try the sea, which he admitted to be more dangerous the narrower it became.

5 · THE PINNACE LOST

Danger was not long away. Around the middle of the night in fact, as the winds were swelling up and the sea became rough, we saw the pinnace at a distance displaying two lights on her masthead. At the time we were certain that she was lost and that she had been swallowed up in the deep whirlpools, for she had passed out of sight in an instant, and no news of her reached us until six weeks later. Therefore everyone was convinced that the pinnace had sunk; however, God had better things in store; for the pinnace, realizing early on that she was no match for the waves, avoided St. George's Channel, against which we were already struggling, and returned to England and the Scilly Isles; making a fresh start from there, she followed us in the company of the *Dragon* to the Great Gulf and caught up with us, as we shall tell, at the Antilles, with God, who cares even for the least, looking out for her as leader and guardian.

6 · THE SHIP ABANDONED TO THE WAVES

But since we were ignorant of this outcome, pain and fear were pressing us hard indeed. The abominable night, full of frequent terrors, increased our fear. At daybreak, though we had the southwest wind blowing against us, we were slowly advancing through many tacks, since [the wind] was rather mild. So Tuesday, Wednesday, and Thursday went by with variable winds and small progress. On Friday, when the south wind prevailed and was driving thick grey clouds together, such a tempest broke forth towards evening, that it seemed that we would be enveloped by the waves with every motion. Nor did the following day, the feast of St. Andrew the Apostle, promise milder weather. The clouds were collecting on all sides in a terrifying manner and, before they finally dispersed, they frightened those gazing at them and created the opinion that all the mischievous storm spirits and evil genii of Maryland had appeared in battle line against us.

7 · THE SUNFISH

Towards evening the captain saw a sunfish striving against the course of the sun, which is indeed a very sure sign of a storm; nor did the omen go unfulfilled. For around ten o'clock at night a dark cloud rained down a violent shower. Such an immense whirlwind had whipped up the rain that it was necessary to furl the sails as rapidly as possible; this could not be done quickly enough to prevent the mainsail, or the bigger sail, the only one with which we were sailing, from being torn from top to bottom. One of its parts was carried away into the sea and was retrieved with difficulty.

8 · THE VOWS AND PRAYERS OF THE CATHOLICS

At this point the spirit of even the bravest, whether passenger or sailor, was alarmed, for they admitted that they had seen tall ships wrecked in a smaller tempest. But this storm kindled the prayers and vows of the Catholics in honor of the Most Blessed Virgin Mother and of her Immaculate Conception, of St. Ignatius, the Patron Saint of Maryland, of St. Michael and of all the guardian angels of that country. And everyone was hastening to purify his soul through the Sacrament of Penance; for when we had lost control over the rudder, the vessel, abandoned to the waves and winds, soon tossed about like a quoit, until God opened a path for her safety. In the beginning, I admit, the fear of losing the ship and my life had seized me; but then I devoted some time to prayer—less tepid than my usual manner—and proposed to the Lord Christ, the Most Blessed Virgin, to St. Ignatius, and to the angels of Maryland that the purpose of this voyage was to honor the blood of our Redeemer through the salvation of the savages, to erect a kingdom for the Savior (if he considered our feeble efforts worthy of assistance), to consecrate another gift to the Immaculate Virgin Mother, and many similar things. After this, a great consolation shone inside my soul, and at the same time such a firm conviction arose that we were to be rescued not only from this, but from every other storm on this voyage, that there was no room for doubt with me. I had given myself to prayer when the sea raged most severely, and (may this be to the glory of God alone) I had barely finished, when I perceived that the storm subsided. This, of course, provided me with a new disposition of spirit and at the same time filled me with enormous joy and wonder, since I felt even more deeply that the will of God was well disposed towards the peoples of Maryland (to whom Your Reverence has sent us). Let the most gentle goodness of our Redeemer be praised in eternity. Amen.

9 • REASSURED OF SAFETY

And so, after the sea had then ceased to rage, the remaining three months' voyage was so very calm, that the captain with his crew asserted that they had never seen a more pleasant or calmer voyage; for we did not suffer an inconvenience of even one hour. But when I speak about three months, I am not saying that we were at sea for so long, but I am counting the whole journey and the stopovers, which we spent on the Antilles; for the voyage itself lasted only seven weeks and two days, and this is considered a quick passage.

10 • FEARS OF THE TURKS

From that time on, therefore, while we were sailing along the coast of Spain, we had neither adverse nor completely favorable wind. Although continuously fearing the [attacks of the] Turks, we came across none of them; perhaps they had withdrawn to celebrate their yearly period of fast, which they actually call *sawm*, for it was taking place at that time of the year. However, when we had sailed past the Straits of Gibraltar and the Madeira Islands, and the winds were filling the sails from the stern (they were not variable any more but stayed fixed towards the south and southwest, which was our course), three ships appeared, one of which surpassed ours in size. They seemed to be about three leagues away towards west and were trying to approach us; and now and then they even seemed to send messengers back and forth to each other and to exchange information. Since we suspected them to be Turkish pirates, we were getting ready all things needed for battle. There were even some among us who urged the captain rather unwisely to provoke and attack them gratuitously; but since he had a master to whom he had to render account, he doubted that he could give a plausible reason for battle. Indeed, I believe that he would have had a difficult confrontation, although they were perhaps as much afraid of us as we were of them. As far as I can infer they were merchants who were making towards the Canary Islands, scattered not far from there, and could not, or did not want to catch up with us.

11 · THE GREAT GULF

Having sailed from this place to the Canary Islands, we were taken up by the great gulf, where there is nothing to be feared unless those on a voyage are running out of provisions because of windless periods at sea, since they sometimes last fifteen days [or even] three weeks. But this happens rarely and barely once or twice in a century; nonetheless, one frequently has to deal with delays because the wind is failing; when it blows, though, it is always constant, and favorable for our voyage. In this gulf we travelled three thousand Italian miles, traversing the billowing sea under full sails, with no calm holding us up, except occasionally for an hour around noon.

12 · WHY THESE FIXED WINDS AND RAINS?

I do not easily find the cause of such a constant wind, except to say that perhaps it arises from the sun's being so near when it passes between the two tropics and with its own force draws two kinds of vapors, one dry from the saltiness of the sea, the other moist by reason of the water: from the former the wind is created, from the latter the rains are produced. The sun, therefore, drawing both of them, is the reason they always keep the same oblique course and constantly follow the sun. And this could also be the reason we experienced intense heat together with abundant rain between the two tropics, constantly in the morning, at noon, and in the evening—or at least [we had] rather violent winds during those hours. Hence the reason can also be deduced why at that time the sea was free from windless periods, for when the sun appears in the Tropic of Capricorn beyond the celestial equator, and swerves to the outermost southern part of the same equator (as it happened when we had been situated between the 13th and 17th degrees, and when in the winter months the heat there is as great as in the summer months in Europe), it obliquely attracts the wind and the rain to the celestial equator; and for that reason the winds are more certain in those months, especially in this gulf and towards the Tropic of Cancer. The windless periods are rather frequent, however, when the sun passes over the equator in the summertime to us and draws salty and watery vapors not at an oblique, but nearly at a right angle.

13 · SICKNESS FROM DRINKING WINE

Here, however, I cannot enough extol the divine goodness, which causes all things to work together for the best for those who love God. For if it had been possible, without the interjected delay, to sail at the time which we had settled upon, namely on the twentieth of August, when the sun on this side of the equator was beating down on the crown of the head, the extreme heat would not only have spoiled the provisions, but would also have brought sickness and death to nearly all of us. The delay was our salvation, for having embarked in the winter time, we avoided misfortunes of this kind; and, if one should except the usual seasickness of seafarers, no one was attacked by disease until the feast of the Nativity of the Lord. Wine was consumed in order that this day might be better celebrated, and those who enjoyed it too intemperately were seized by fever the following day; they were thirty in number, and from those about twelve died not very much later, including two Catholics, Nicholas Fairfax and James Barefoot, [which] left with everyone great grief over their loss.

14 • FLYING FISH. TROPICAL BIRDS

While we were sailing, many curious things were happening: especially fish about as big as sparling fish, or smelt, that at times were passing through the sea, at times on wings high through the air, and are said to have a very pleasant taste. A hundred together rise in crowds into the air, when they flee from pursuing dolphins. Some of them fell into our ship, when the oars of their wings failed them, for in one leap they do not fly through a space of more than two or three acres; then, when their wings have dried out by beating the air, they plunge back into the water before venturing again into the sky. When we were twenty-one degrees and a few minutes away from the equator, where the tropic begins, we saw birds hovering in the air, which they call "tropical" birds after the location. They equal a falcon in size and are striking because of two very long, white feathers in their tail; it is uncertain whether they remain constantly in the air, or whether they sometimes rest themselves on the water. The remaining things I omit as being known already through the letters of others.

15 • BONAVISTA ABOUNDS IN SALT AND GOATS

When we had sailed past the Canary Islands, Lord Leonard Calvert, the commander of the fleet, began to consider which goods should be loaded on the ship for her return, and where they were to be had, so that through this he might take care of the expenses of his brother, Baron Baltimore; for the whole burden fell to him as the initiator of the entire voyage. We were expecting no advantage from our countrymen in Virginia, for they are hostile to this new settlement. Therefore we were heading towards St. Christopher; fearing, after some deliberation, that in this late season of the year others might have come before us, we turned the ship southward to reach Bonavista; this island is situated opposite of Angola on the African coast, 14 degrees from the equator and is a post of the Dutch; they collect salt there which they then either transfer home or use in Greenland to preserve fish. The abundance of salt and also of goats, of which the island is prolific, tempted us; for otherwise it does not have any inhabitants. Only a few Portuguese, banished into exile because of their crimes, drag out their lives there as well as they can. We had barely covered two hundred miles, when at someone's suggestion our plans were changed again, and so that we might not run out of provisions by travelling in such a roundabout way, we turned towards Barbados.

16 · BARBADOS. SUPPLIES DEAR

This is the lowest of the Caribbean or Antilles Islands, only 13 degrees distant from the equator, and the granary of the other islands (which stretch in the manner of an arch in a long line up to the Gulf of Mexico). As we reached it on the third of January, we came expecting many articles of trade from the English inhabitants and the governor, a brother [of one of the participants in the expedition]; but they had conspired against us and resolved to sell a bushel of wheat, which normally sold on the island for half a Belgian florin, for five times the amount, i.e., for two florins and a half. They were offering a suckling pig at fifty florins, a turkey for twenty-five, and other smaller fowl of that kind for three florins; they did not have any beef or mutton; for they live on corn-bread and potatoes, and this type of root grows in such abundance that it is possible to carry off entire carts for free.

17 · DIVINE PROVIDENCE

The consideration of Divine Providence mitigated the harsh severity of men, for we learned that a Spanish fleet stood at the island of Bonavista in order to keep all foreigners from the salt trade. If we had further hastened on the route decided upon earlier, we would have fallen as prey into the trap. However, we were rescued from a greater danger at Barbados. The slaves throughout the island had conspired to kill their masters; then, after freeing themselves, they had evidently decided to get possession of the first ship which landed and to take to the sea. The conspiracy had been revealed by someone frightened by the fierceness of the deed, and the punishment of one of the ringleaders restored security to the island, and safety to us; for our ship, as the one which first was laid to the shore, had been determined as prey, and on the very day we landed we found eight hundred men in arms with the purpose of opposing this most recent crime.

18 • INTENSE HEAT. HAMMOCKS. COTTON

It is pleasing to describe some wonderful things which this island brings forth. The island is thirty miles long and fifteen miles wide, is thirteen degrees away from the equator, and has such high temperatures that the inhabitants are dressed in linen clothes during the winter months and immerse themselves rather frequently in the waters. When we arrived, it was the time of harvest. Habitation would be impossible, unless frequent winds tempered the heat. Their beds are blankets of cloth, skillfully woven out of cotton. When it is time to rest they sleep in this cloth, after it has been hung by ropes from poles on each side. At daytime, on the other hand, they carry it off wherever it pleases them. The chief articles of trade are grain and cotton. It is pleasant to see the manner and abundance of cotton hanging from the tree. The tree from which it grows is not taller than Oxyacanthus (which the people call barberry), although it is more like a tree than a shrub. It bears a walnut-sized pod, which is rather pointed in shape, divided into four parts, and gives forth cotton whiter than snow and softer than a feather, rolled up in the shape of a nut. Six small seeds similar to vetch rest upon the cotton; when it has been collected and separated from the seed by means of a kind of wheel, they store it in sacks and preserve it.

19 • A HUGE CABBAGE

Particularly admirable is a type of cabbage, which, although it has a stalk growing to the height of one hundred and eighty feet, is eaten either raw or boiled. The stalk itself down to one foot under the fruit is considered a delicacy. Eaten raw, with pepper added, it surpasses the artichoke in taste, and is closer to a peeled walnut. The huge stalk easily equals the trunk of a big tree, yet it is no tree nonetheless, but a leguminous plant, and bears no more than one cabbage. In the same place one can also see a sufficiently tall tree which they call the soap tree. The seeds do not exceed a hazelnut in size; their covering is oily; it cleans and cleanses like soap, although, as they say, it is detrimental to more delicate linen. I have carried off many of these kernels with me to Maryland and planted in the earth the seeds of future trees.

20 • THE PALM OF CHRIST. GUAVA. PAPAW. PINEAPPLE

They also count the Palm of Christ among their trees, although it has a trunk that is porous and similar to a leguminous plant. It brings forth an immense cluster of ash-colored seeds, armed with thorns and sprinkled with dark spots. From these an excellent oil is pressed. Oranges, lemons, pomegranates, even nuts which the Spanish call "coconuts", and the remaining fruits of the hot regions come up abundantly.

There is also a fruit which is called guava, of golden color and in the shape of a rather small lemon; in taste, however, it resembles the quince. The papaw is not unlike it in color and shape, but since it is very sweet, it is only used to give taste to foods.

The pineapple, however, surpasses all other fruits that I have tasted elsewhere in the world. It is of golden color mixed with a most pleasant green and equals three or four European nuts of the same name in size. It is not completely unlike them in shape, but more elaborate, not with so many separate cells and divisions, which reveal the kernel when applied to fire, but soft and enveloped by a thin skin. Most delightful in taste, it does not have a rough seed, but pleases the palate equally from the top downwards; nor does it lack the crown which it deserves; for without a doubt it can be called the queen of fruit. It has an aromatic taste, which I would say resembles strawberries mixed with wine and sugar. It contributes very much to preserving one's health, and agrees so well with the constitution of the body that, though it corrodes iron, it nonetheless strengthens man more than anything else; you will not find it on a high tree, but one fruit growing out of one root like an artichoke. I wished I could send one fruit into the hands of Your Paternity with this letter, for nothing besides the fruit itself can describe it according to its merit.

21 • SANTA LUCIA. MARTINIQUE. ANTILLES OR CARIB ISLANDS

On the twenty-fourth day of January, at night, we weighed anchor and, having passed Santa Lucia at our left around noon of the following day, we reached Martinique towards evening. Here two boats of naked men were offering melons, gourds, fruits of the plane tree, and parrots for barter, from afar though, since they were afraid of the size of our ship. They are a savage people, tall, plump, shining with dark red paint, ignorant of divinity; they practice cannibalism and had consumed several interpreters of the English a while ago. They inhabit an especially fertile region, but one which is all forest and has no accessible plain. After we had displayed a white flag at the stern as a sign of peace, we invited those who were showing themselves from afar to trade; but having turned away from our sign, they demanded that we show them the usual colors [indicating our nationality]. When we had shown them, and they understood who we were, they took courage and came closer, but, having accepted only a few bells and little knives, and because they did not much trust the very powerful ship, they approached the pinnace and promised that they would bring better goods on the next day, if we decided to stay. Some day, I hope, someone will have compassion for this forsaken people. With the sailors a rumor spread (originating from some shipwrecked Frenchmen) that an animal can be found on this island on whose forehead sits a stone of uncommon splendor, similar to a glowing coal, or a burning candle. To this animal they gave the name "Carbuncle". Let the originator be responsible for the proof of this matter.

22 · GUADALUPE. MONSERRAT. NEVIS. ST. CHRISTOPHER

When the next day was dawning, we reached another Caribbean island, which is named after Guadaloupe in Spain because of the similarity created by its rough mountains, and is, as I am assured, also under the protection of the Most Holy Virgin Mother. From there we reached Montserrat around noon, where we learned from a French cutter that we were not yet safe from the fleet of the Spanish. Montserrat has Irish inhabitants who had been driven out of Virginia by the English because of the profession of their Catholic faith. Then we came to Nevis, which is infamous because of its unhealthy air and fevers. After we had spent one day there, we set sail to St. Christopher, where we stayed for ten days, since we were invited in a friendly manner by the English governor and two Catholic captains. The governor of the French colony on the same island received me with especial generosity.

23 · A SULPHUR MOUNTAIN. THE VIRGIN PLANT. THE LOCUST TREE AND FRUIT

Whatever rare things are seen at Barbados, I have also found here; and besides [those], not far from the residence of the governor, a sulphur mountain and something one may wonder at even more, the virgin plant, so called because at the smallest touch of a finger it begins to droop immediately and collapses, and yet, when it has had time to recover, it revives and stands up again. The locust tree pleased me especially, which is supposed to have offered nourishment to St. John the Baptist; it equals an elm tree in height, and is so pleasant to the bees that they most willingly entwine their honeycombs within it. The honey, if you took away the label "wild", differs neither in color nor flavor from the purest I have tasted. The fruit, which is also called "locust", contains supple but firm flesh inside the harder rind, equal to six pods of beans, and is in taste similar to meal mixed with honey; it bears four or five rather large, chestnut-colored seeds. I have carried off several of them to be planted [in Maryland].

24 • CAPE COMFORT IN VIRGINIA

And so when we finally sailed from here, we reached the cape, that they call Cape Comfort, in Virginia on the 27th of February, filled with fear that the English inhabitants, to whom our settlement was completely unwelcome, might contrive some evil against us. However, the letter which we were carrying from the King and the supreme treasurer to the governor of those regions was very effective in appeasing their minds, and enabled us to obtain things that would be useful to us in the future. For the governor of Virginia was hoping that through this kindness toward us, he would more easily recover from the royal treasury a great sum of money which was due to him. They only announced to us that a rumor had been spread that six ships were approaching, in order to bring everything under the power of the Spanish, and that the natives were in arms because of this —which indeed we found to be true afterwards. The rumor, however, had originated with the English, I am afraid.

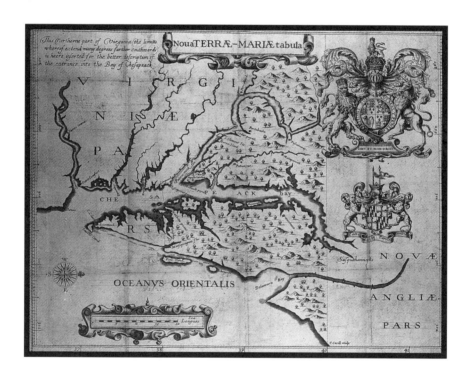

25 • CHESAPEAKE BAY.
POTOMAC, OR ST. GREGORY'S RIVER.
CAPE ST. MICHAEL

After eight or nine days of generous treatment we set sail on the third of March and, having travelled into Chesapeake Bay, we turned our course to the north, in order to reach the Potomac River. Chesapeake Bay flows gently between the shores; it is ten leagues wide, four, five, six, and seven fathoms deep, and teeming with fish, when it is the right time of the year. You will hardly find a more pleasant, evenly flowing river. Nonetheless, it yields to the Potomac River, which we named after St. Gregory.

Since we had already reached the desired region, we distributed names according to the circumstances. And in fact we dedicated the promontory, which is located towards the south, to the honor of St. Gregory, the northern one to St. Michael, naming it so in honor of all the angels of Maryland. I have never seen a greater and more delightful river; compared to it the Thames seems a mere rivulet. It is not tainted by swamps, but on both sides wonderful forests of fine trees rise up on solid ground, not made inaccessible by thornhedges and underbrush, but just as if planted spaciously by hand so that one could easily drive a chariot drawn by four horses between the trees.

26 • THE FEAR AND WONDER OF THE NATIVES. THE HERON ISLANDS. LINEN LOST

At the mouth of the river itself we perceived armed natives. That night fires were burning in the entire region, and, since such a big ship had never been seen by them, messengers sent from this side and from that were reporting that a canoe similar to an island had come near, and that it held as many men as there are trees in the woods. We, however, continued to the Heron Islands, so called from the unheard of throngs of this kind of bird. The first one [island] in our way we named after St. Clement; the second after St. Catherine; the third after St. Cecilia. We first left the ship at St. Clement's Island, to which no access lay open except through a shallow because of the sloping shore. Here the maids, who had left the ship to wash the laundry, almost drowned, when the skiff turned over, and a great part of my linen clothes were lost, no small loss in these parts.

This island abounds in cedar, sassafras, herbs and flowers to make all kinds of salads, also in a wild nut tree which bears a very hard nut, with a thick shell and a small but wonderfully tasty kernel. However, since it is only four hundred acres wide, it did not seem spacious enough as a location for the new settlement. Nonetheless, a place was sought to build a fort to prevent strangers from trafficking on the river and to guard the territory, for this was the shortest way across the river.

27 • THE FIRST MASS. A CROSS ERECTED

On the day of the Annunciation of the Most Holy Virgin Mary we celebrated mass for the first time in this island: this had never been done before in this region of the world. When mass was over, we took an enormous cross, which we had hewn out of a tree, on our shoulders, proceeded in rank to a designated place and, with the help of the governor, his associates, and the remaining Catholics, erected a monument to Christ, our Savior, while we humbly recited the Litany of the Holy Cross on bended knee, with much emotion.

28 • INTERVIEW WITH THE CHIEFTAIN OF POTOMAC AND THE PARAMOUNT CHIEF [AT PISCATAWAY]

When the governor had understood, however, that several rulers were subject to the emperor of Piscataway, he decided to approach him, so that, when he had explained the cause of our voyage and won over his good will, we might have easier access to the minds of the others. Therefore he joined another ship, which he had procured in Virginia, to our pinnace [the *Dove*], left the ship [the *Ark*] anchored at St. Clement's, and having turned around his course, went ashore on the southern part of the river. When he learned that the savages had fled inland, he advanced to the city, which, having taken its name from the river, is also called Potomac. Since the king was still a boy, his uncle, a dignified and prudent man by the name of Archihu, was his guardian and ruled in his place. He gladly lent his ear to our Father Altham, who had been added as a companion to the governor (who was, indeed, still keeping me back with the cargo) and explained through an interpreter some things about the errors of the pagans, while Archihu acknowledged his own repeatedly. When he had been fully informed that we had not landed there to make war but on account of good will, so that we might instruct a rough people with civilized precepts and open them the path to heaven, he indicated that we were welcome. The interpreter was one of the Protestants of Virginia. And so, since Father could not discuss more at the time, he promised that he would return not much later. "This is just what I want," said Archihu, "we will share one table, my followers will also go hunting for you, and all things will be in common between us."

From there they went to Piscataway, where all had come together in arms. About five hundred men armed with bows had taken a stand with the paramount chief. After signs of peace had been given, the chieftain, having laid aside his fear, came on board the pinnace, and when he had heard of our kind intentions toward this people, he gave us permission to settle in whichever part of his territory we wished.

In the meantime, while the governor was on his trip to the chieftain, the savages at St. Clement's had become bolder and too familiar with our guards. For we were keeping watch night and day, to protect at one time our woodcutters against sudden attacks, at another the boat which we were building, since it had been brought here with its boards and ribs disassembled. It was a pleasure to hear them wonder about each item: especially where in the world such a big tree had grown, that such a huge mass of a ship was hewn from it; for they believed that it had been cut out of the trunk of one tree, just like an Indian canoe. The larger cannons were holding them in astonishment: certainly they were more resounding than their hissing bows, and equal to thunder.

29 • ST. MARY'S CITY. ST. GEORGE'S RIVER. AUGUSTA CAROLINA

The governor on his way to the chieftain had employed as his companion Captain Henry Fleet, one of those who live in Virginia, a man especially welcome to the savages, fluent in the language, and acquainted with the region. In the beginning he was a very close friend; later on, misled by the evil plans of a certain Claiborne, he became very hostile and incited the minds of the natives against us by every means he could. In the meantime, however, while he acted as a friend among us, he pointed out to the governor such a charming place for a settlement that Europe can hardly offer a better one. Thus, when we had advanced from St. Clement's about nine leagues, we sailed into the mouth of a river, which we had named after St. George, on the northern side [of the Potomac]. This river runs forward from south to north about twenty miles before it is absorbed by the salt water from the sea, [and in this it is] not unlike the Thames. In its mouth one can see two bays, able to hold 300 ships of huge size. One bay we dedicated to St. George, the other one, more inward, to the Most Blessed Virgin Mary. The left side of the river was the seat of the king of Yaocomico. We went up from the coast inland on the right side, and about a thousand paces removed from the shore, we gave the name of St. Mary to the designated city, and in order to prevent any pretext for injury or occasion for enmity, we bought thirty miles of that land from the chieftain in exchange for hatchets, axes, hoes and some amount of cloth. This region already has the name of Augusta Carolina.

30 · THE SUSQUEHANNOCKS

The Susquehannocks, a people used to waging war and dangerous above all to the king of Yaocomico, lays waste to every field during frequent attacks, and forces the inhabitants to seek other places of settlement out of fear of this danger. This is the reason we so quickly obtained a part of this kingdom, with God opening a path for His law and eternal light through His support. Daily several [natives] depart and leave us their houses, fields, and crops. This is indeed similar to a miracle, that the savage people, only a few days before prepared in arms [to war] against us, yielded to us easily like lambs, and handed over themselves and their belongings. This is the finger of God, and God intends some great benefit for this people. At this time a few are yet allowed to live among us now until the next year. Then, however, the area is to be left to us.

31 · THE NATIVES. THEIR DRESS. HOUSES

The natives are of tall and fine stature, with naturally dark skin, which they generally make more shocking by painting it with a specially prepared red oil in order to keep away the gnats; thus they are more intent on comfort than on appearance. They also disfigure their faces with other colors, blue from the nose upwards, red downwards, or the reverse, in various and really horrible ways. And, since they lack a beard nearly to extreme old age, they paint on a beard with lines of variable color, drawn from the outermost lips to the ears. They tie their hair, which is commonly black, pulled around with a band into a knot at the left ear, and also add some ornament which is of value with them. Some wear the shape of a fish in copper on the forehead. They surround their necks with glass beads connected by a thread in the manner of a necklace, although these beads are beginning to be of little worth to them and [are] less and less useful for trade.

They are dressed for the most part in deerskins, or in a covering of similar kind, which flows from the back in the manner of a mantle; around the middle of the body they wear an apron, otherwise they are naked. The young boys and girls wander about without any covering. With the soles of their feet, which are hard like horn, they tread prickles and thorny plants without being hurt. Their weapons are a bow and arrows, which are two cubits long and equipped with [a tip made of] an antler, or a very sharp white flintstone. They shoot these arrows with such great skill that they pierce a sparrow through the middle from a distance; and in order to practice [to achieve] skill they throw a thong of leather into the air, then they release an arrow from the bowstring and pierce the thong before it falls down. But since they use a bow that is not quite tightly strung, they cannot hit a target when it is situated very far away. By means of these weapons they live, and daily they hunt squirrels, partridges, turkeys, and other animals throughout the fields and forests. There is a vast abundance of all these animals, although we, from fear of an ambush, do not yet dare to provide food for us ourselves by hunting.

They inhabit houses built in an oval, oblong shape, and nine or ten feet high. Light is admitted into them through a window, which is one cubit long; it also serves to carry off the smoke; for they kindle a fire in the middle of the floor and sleep around the fire. Their chieftains, however, and foremost men have their own chambers and a bed with four posts driven into the earth and covered by poles placed over them. One of these cottages fell to me and my companions. We are housed sufficiently comfortably in it for the time, until more spacious buildings may be built. You may call it the first chapel of Maryland, although it is quite a bit more properly furnished than when it used to be inhabited by the Indians. With the next voyage, if God should favor our undertaking, our people will not lack the other things necessary and useful in houses.

32 · THEIR CHARACTER. FOOD

The character of the people is noble and cheerful, and they understand well when a matter is proposed to them. They have excellent senses of taste and smell, and they excel even the Europeans in eyesight. They live for the most part on a mush, which they call pone, and hominy. Both are made from corn, and they add at times fish, or whatever they have obtained by hunting and fowling. They avoid wine and warm drinks as much as possible and are not easily induced to taste them, except for those whom the English have corrupted with their vices. With regard to chastity, I declare that I have not yet perceived in a man or a woman any action which savored of inconstancy, yet they are with us and near us every day and take pleasure in our company. They hasten toward us of their own accord with a cheerful expression and offer us what they have obtained by hunting or fishing, sometimes also cakes and boiled or roasted oysters, and this they do when they have been invited with a few words of their language, which we have so far learned through signs. They marry several wives, yet they keep conjugal faith inviolate. The appearance of the women is dignified and modest. They sustain a generous spirit toward everyone; whatever kindness you may confer on them they return. They decide nothing rashly or seized by a sudden passion, but by reason. When, therefore, anything of importance is proposed at any time, they are silent for a while and think it over; then they either briefly agree or refuse, and they are very tenacious of their resolution. Truly, if once they should be instructed in Christian precepts (and indeed nothing seems to stand in the way besides our ignorance of the language used in these parts), they will become outstanding observers of virtue and humanity. They are held by a wonderful desire for civilized intercourse and European garments, and they would already long ago have used [European] clothing, if the greed of the merchants, who exchange cloth only for beaver pelts, had not stood in the way. But not everyone can hunt beaver. Far be it from us to imitate the greed of these men.

33 · RELIGION

Our ignorance of the language is the reason that it is not quite certain what they in turn think about religion, for we do not fully trust our Protestant interpreters. These few things we have hurriedly learned: they acknowledge a God of the sky, whom they call our God; however, they do not offer him any external honor. But they try to appease by every means a certain evil spirit whom they call Ochre, so that he may not harm them. As I hear, they worship grain and fire as wonderfully beneficial to humankind. Some of our group relate that they have seen the following ceremony in the temple of the Patuxent. On the appointed day all men and women of all ages, from several districts, gathered around an enormous fire. Closest to the fire the young ones were standing, behind them those more advanced in age. Then some deer fat was thrown into the fire and with hands and voices raised to heaven they were all crying out: "taho taho." After an interval someone brings a large bag. In this bag is a pipe and powder, which they call "potre." The pipe is similar to the kind our countrymen use to inhale smoke, but much bigger. The bag then is carried around the fire, while the boys and girls follow and alternate in a sufficiently pleasant voice: "taho taho." When the circle has been completed, the pipe is taken out of the bag, and the powder potre is distributed to each individual standing by. It is lighted, and everyone inhales its smoke through the pipe and blows it over the several members of his body and consecrates them. It was not possible to learn more, except that they seem to have some notion of a flood, by which the earth perished because of the crimes of mankind.

34 • THE SOIL

We have been here only one month, and so further information must be sent by the next ship. I declare [however] that the soil seems especially fertile. Far and wide in the very dense forests we tread on strawberries, vines, sassafras, acorns, and nuts. Soft, black earth of about one foot is spread over rich, dense red clay. Very high trees are everywhere, except where a field is cultivated by a few people. An abundance of springs supplies drink. No other mammals appear besides deer, beaver, and squirrels, which compare in size to European hares. Infinite is the number of birds of various colors, such as eagles, herons, swans, geese, partridges, and ducks. On account of this one can infer that this region does not lack the sort of things that serve the convenience and pleasure of its inhabitants.

Relatio Itineris in Marilandiam

LATIN TEXT

vigesimus = vicesimus, -a, um — twentieth
mensis November (-bris), m. — November
die Sanctae Ceciliae sacro — 'on St. Cecilia's Day'
aspiro, 1 — to blow
eurus, -i — southeast or east wind
solvimus — 'we sailed'. Between 131 and 148 passengers participated in the expedition, travelling aboard two ships, the *Ark*, a large ship of about three hundred tons, and the pinnace *Dove*, a much smaller vessel of about thirty tons.
insula Vecta — the Isle of Wight
praecipuus, -a, -um — main, principal
constituo, 3, -stitui, -stitutum — to place
tutela, -ae — protection
Sancti Ignatii — St. Ignatius of Loyola (1491-1556) was the founder of the Society of Jesus, or Jesuits, the religious order to which three of the passengers, including Father White, belonged.
angelus, -i — angel
Marilandia, -ae — Maryland. The colony was named after the Queen of Charles I, Henrietta Maria.
paululum — a little
provehor, -vehi — to be conveyed, sail, advance
deficio, 3 — to become weak, fail
resido, 3, -sedi, -sessum — to cast anchor, stop
e regione — opposite (of)
castrum Yaremouth — Yarmouth Castle
ad occasum aestivum — 'toward the summer sunset', 'toward the northwest'. In the summer the sun is going down somewhere between west and north. Yarmouth Castle is on the northwestern coast of the Isle of Wight.
inter duas terras — 'between the two shores' [of the Isle of Wight and mainland England]
festus, -a, -um — festive, public
tormentum, -i — piece of artillery, cannon
tonitruum, -i — thunder; here: salute (of artillery)
excepti fuimus = excepti sumus
neque tamen metus aberat — during the religious strife of the sixteenth and seventeenth centuries, religious minorities all over Europe had reason to live in fear. In England, Roman Catholics suffered increasingly harsh repression. The Maryland colony, however, was to provide not only a safe haven for Catholics, but religious freedom for all denominations; the expedition described by Father White included Protestants as well as Catholics.
mussito, 1 — to grumble, mutter
expectare = exspectare
Londino — from London
nuntius, -ii — messenger, message
necto, 3 — to devise
Nautae ... videbantur — since the opponents of the expedition, particularly those with interests in Virginia, had already caused a delay of three months, it is not improbable that they continued their attempts to prevent the expedition, as Father White suggests.
abrumpo, -rumpere, -rupi, -ruptum — to break off, destroy
quippe — indeed
prosperus, -a, -um — favorable, lucky
validus, -a, -m — powerful
lembus, -i — cutter (a small, swift vessel)
Gallicus, -a, -um — French
consto, 1 -stiti, statum — to stand together, moor together
prope abfuit in nostram celocem ut impingeret — 'came very close to running into our pinnace'
celox, -ocis, f. — pinnace (a light sailing vessel). The narrator, Father White, was not on board the pinnace, but made the voyage on board the *Ark* and was probably watching the events described here from afar.
opprimo, 3 — to crush, smother
una — in one, together, at once
praecido, 3 -cidi, -cisum — to cut away
deperdo = perdo, -ere, -didi, -ditum — to lose
anchora, -ae — anchor
vela dare — 'we set sail'. The present infinitive is used for vivid description of past events, in Roman literature especially by Sallust and Tacitus.
quamprimum — as fast as possible
eo loci = eo loco
fluctuo, 1 — to float
porro — forward, further
demitto, 3 — to lower, bring down = sail downstream
decerno, 3 — to decide
agito, 1 — to consider, discuss, be engaged upon
dissipo, 1 — to scatter, disperse

RELATIO ITINERIS IN MARILANDIAM

1 · SOLVUNT A CONIS

Vigesimo secundo mensis Novembris anni 1633 die Sanctae Ceciliae sacro, leniter aspirante euro, solvimus a Conis, qui portus est in insula Vecta. Cumque praecipuas partes navis constituissemus in tutela Dei in primis et Sanctissimae eius Matris, Sancti Ignatii et omnium angelorum Marilandiae, paululum inter duas terras provecti, deficiente vento, resedimus e regione castri Yaremouth, quod est ad occasum aestivum eiusdem insulae. Hic festis tormentorum tonitruis excepti fuimus; neque tamen metus aberat. Nautae enim inter se mussitabant expectare se Londino nuntium et litteras, atque ideo moras etiam nectere videbantur. Sed Deus consilia adversa abrupit. Eadem quippe nocte, prospero sed valido flante vento, lembus Gallicus (qui eodem portu nobiscum constiterat) solvere coactus prope abfuit in nostram celocem ut impingeret. Illa igitur, ne opprimeretur, una praecisa ac deperdita anchora, vela dare quamprimum; et quoniam eo loci fluctuare periculosum erat, in mare porro se demittere festinat. Itaque ne celocis nostrae conspectum perderemus, sequi decernimus. Ita quae nautae in nos agitarunt consilia sunt dissipata.

1 Hoc anno etiam expeditio a nostris in Marilandiam instituta *manus altera addidit in marg. sup.* 6 Solvunt a Conis *in marg. dext.*

ACUS glossary (first)

die Sancto Clementi sacro — 'on St. Clement's Day'
alligo, 1 — tie to, bind to
mergo 3, mersi, mersum — to plunge into, immerse
corona, -ae — crown
martirium -ii — martyrdom
adipiscor, 3 adeptus sum (dep.) — to obtain
praebeo, 2, praebui, praebitum — to offer, provide, show
enarro, 1 — to narrate, explain
mirabilis, -e — wonderful, extraordinary

ACUS

[hora] matutina, -ae — morning hour
festivus, -a -um — cheerful, festive
explosio, -onis, f. — salute shooting
saluto, 1 — to greet
castrum, -i — castle
frequens, -ntis — numerous
scopulus, -i — rock, cliff
Acus, -uum — the Needles (rock formation at the western end of the Isle of Wight)
terror, -oris, m. — fright, terror
duplex, -icis — double, two-fold
aestus, -us, m. — raging, surf, tide
hinc — on this side
illhinc = illinc — on that side
vicinus, -a, -um — neighboring, on the other side
littus = litus, -oris, n. — shore, coast
abripio, -ere — to drag off, snatch away
allido, 3 — to dash against
abripientem, allidentem : modify aestum
ut taceam — 'to say nothing of'
interim — meanwhile, however
discrimen, -inis, n. — danger
defungor, -fungi, -functum with abl. — to deal with, overcome, have done with
urgeo, 2 — to push, press, drive
nondum recepta achora — 'since we had not yet weighed anchor' (= pulled up the anchor)
haereo, 2 — to hang to, hang on, remain fixed
prope erat...allideretur — 'the ship would nearly have been dashed against the shore'
subitus, -a, -um — sudden
aversus, -a, -um — turned away
immergo, 3 — to plunge in, immerse
propitius, -a, -um — favorable, gracious
Deo propitio — 'by the grace of God'
eludo, -ere, -lusi, -lusum — to evade, escape
pignus, -oris, n. — pledge, token, proof
dignor, -ari, -atus sum with abl. — to consider worthy of
meritum, -i, — merit

INSULAE SILLINAE

in Sabbatum incidit — 'fell on a Sabbath' (= Saturday)
insequenti = sequenti (abl. sing.)
posterus, -a, -um — following, next
mane — in the morning, early
a tergo — behind (us)
promontorium, ii — promontory
Anglia, ae — England
occiduus, -a, -um — western
placidus, -a, -um — quiet, gentle, smooth
cursus, -us, m. — course, movement, journey, sailing
in occasum — towards the west
lego, 3 — to traverse, pass through

Accidit id 23 Novembris die Sancto
35 Clementi sacro, qui anchora alligatus et
in mare mersus coronam martirii
adeptus est, et iter praebuit populo
terrae ut enarrent mirabilia Dei.

2 · ACUS

40 Eo igitur die iterum, circa decimam
matutinam, festivis explosionibus
salutati a castro Hurst, praetervecti
sumus frequentes scopulos ad extremum insulae Vectae, quos a forma Acus
45 vocant. Sunt autem navigantibus
terrori, propter duplicem aestum maris,
hinc in saxa, illhinc in vicinum littus
abripientem et allidentem naves, ut
alterum interim discrimen taceam, quo
50 defuncti sumus ad castrum Yaremouth.
Nam vento et aestu urgente, cum
nondum recepta anchora haereremus,
prope erat ut navis ad terram allideretur,
nisi subito vi magna aversi, eam mari
55 immergentes, periculum, Deo propitio,
elusissemus, qui hoc etiam pignore
protectionis suae nos dignatus est per
merita Sancti Clementis.

3 · INSULAE SILLINAE

60 Die illo, qui in Sabbatum incidit, et
nocte insequenti ventis usi sumus ita
secundis ut postero die mane, circa
horam nonam, reliquerimus a tergo
promontorium Angliae occiduum et
65 insulas Sillinas, placido cursu magis
in occasum versi, legentes oceanum

---

44 Acus *in marg. sin.* **62** Insulae Sillinae *in marg sin.*

oceanus Britannicus, -i — the English Channel
accelero, 1 — to hasten
celox, -ocis, f. — pinnace
celocem praecurrentes — 'getting ahead of the pinnace'
plus nimio — 'too much'
infesto, 1 — to infest, make dangerous
Turcae, -arum — the Turks
pirata, -ae — pirate
hinc — thereupon, then
oneraria, -ae — merchant ship
oneraria insignis vasorum sexcentorum — 'a merchant ship of six hundred tons'
cui nomen a Dracone datum est — 'which was named *Dragon*', 'by the name of *Dragon*'
Angola, -ae — Angola. Now independent, Angola was at one time a Portuguese colony in southwest Africa
pomeridianus = postmeridianus, -a, -um — of the afternoon
assequor, 3 (dep.) — to reach by following, come up to, overtake
perfungor, -fungi, functus sum, with abl. — to go through, endure
admitto, 3 — to allow
vacat — there is free time
cursus, -us — running, course, movement, journey
clangor, -oris, m. — sound, noise
tuba, -ae — trumpet
integer, -gra, -grum — entire, whole
contendo, 3 — to compete
arrideo = adrideo, 2 — to be favorable to
quamvis siparo non uteremur — 'although we did not use the topsail'
sisto, 3 — to stop
conspectui nostro se subduxit — 'passed out of sight'

IACTATE TEMPESTATE

die Dominica...Novembris — 'on Sunday, the 24th of November'
die Lunae 25 — 'on Monday the 25th'
prosper, -era, -erum — favorable, fair
navigatio, -onis, f. — sailing
aquilo, -onis, m. — northwind; north
obverto, -vertere, -verti, -versum — to turn toward
exorior, -oriri, -ortus sum (dep.) — to arise
oneraria, -ae — merchant ship
retrotraho, -ere, -traxi, -tractum — to reverse, retrace
Anglia, -ae — England
portus, -us, m. — port, harbour
Paumonii, -iorum — Falmouth (port on the southwestern coast of England)
celeber, -bris, -bre — frequented, much resorted to
repeto, -ere, -petivi, petitum — to seek
repetierit = repetiverit
* celox, -ocis, f. — pinnace
vasorum tantum 40 — 'a vessel of only 40 tons'
adnavigo, 1 — to sail near
naufragium, -ii — shipwreck
charchesium, -ii — masthead (the top of a mast)
significo, 1 — to indicate
vehor, vehi — to be carried, advance, sail
validus, -a, -um — strong

Britannicum, neque quantum potuissemus accelerantes ne, celocem plus nimio praecurrentes, illa Turcis et

70 piratis mare illud plerumque infestantibus praeda fieret.

Hinc factum est ut oneraria insignis vasorum sexcentorum, cui nomen a Dracone datum est, cum Londino

75 profecta Angolam peteret, nos circa tertiam pomeridianam assequeretur. Et quoniam periculo perfunctis voluptatis iam aliquid admittere vacabat, iucundum erat spectare has duas naves

80 inter se cursu et tubarum clangore per horam integram contendentes, caelo et ventis arridentibus. Et superasset nostra, quamvis siparo non uteremur, nisi sistendum fuisset propter celocem,

85 quae tardior erat; itaque cessimus onerariae; illa autem ante vesperam praetervecta conspectui nostro se subduxit.

4 · IACTATE TEMPESTATE

90 Die igitur Dominico 24 et die Lunae et 25 Novembris usque ad vesperam prospera usi sumus navigatione. Tum vero ventis in aquilonem obversis, tanta exorta est tempestas ut oneraria, quam

95 dixi, Londinensis, retrotracto cursu, Angliam et portum apud Paumonios celebrem repetierit. Celox etiam nostra, vasorum tantum 40 cum esset, viribus coepit diffidere et adnavigans monuit

100 se, si naufragium metueret, id luminibus charchesio ostensis significaturam. Vehebamur interim nos valida navi

---

70 pyratis *ms* **91** Iactati tempestate *in marg. sin.*

lignum, -i — wood, timber
construo, 3 — to build
navarchus, -i — captain
optio, -onis, f. — choice
porro — further, again
colluctor, 1 (dep.) — to struggle, contend
littus (-oris, n.) Hibernicum — the Irish coast
caecus, -a, -um — hidden
scopulus, -i — rock, cliff
frequens, -ntis — frequent
infamis, -e — infamous
probo, 1 — to prove, show, test
tracto, 1 — to handle, manage
sedit animo — 'he decided'
angustus, -a , -um — narrow

CELOX PERDITA

turgeo, 2 — to swell up
exaspero, 1 — to make rough
videre erat = vidimus
protendo, 3 — to stretch forward, display
scilicet — evidently, certainly
actum de illa esse — 'that she was done for', 'that she was lost'
haurio, -ire, hausi, haustum, — to swallow up
vortex, -icis, m. — whirl, whirlpool
existimo, 1 — to believe
momentum, -i — moment
conspectus, -us, m. — sight
neque nisi — 'and not until'
septimana, -ae — week
aliquid — here: 'any news'
emano, 1 — here: 'to reach'
cunctis erat persuasum — 'everyone was convinced'
provideo, -ere, -vidi, -visum — to provide for, have in store for
impar, -is — unequal, ill-matched, no match for
mature — in good time, early
oceanus Virginius (= Verginius, or Vergivius) — 'the Virginian Sea'
(the southern part of St. George's Channel off the coast of the counties Waterford and Wexford, Ireland)
devito, 1 — to avoid
unde postliminio — 'making a fresh start from there'
Dracone comite — 'in the company of the *Dragon*' (the ship which the *Ark* had been racing earlier on)
sinus, -us, m. — gulf
insulae Antillae — the Antilles, or West Indies
assequor, assequi, assecutus sum — to reach by following, catch up with
exiguus, -a, -um — small, little

vasorum quadringentorum, neque
aptior ex ligno et ferro construi poterat.
105 Navarcho utebamur peritissimo; data
est itaque illi optio redeundi, si vellet, in
Angliam, vel cum ventis porro colluctandi, quibus si cederet, expectabat nos
e proximo littus Hibernicum caecis
110 scopulis et frequentissimis naufragiis
infame. Vicit tamen navarchi audax
animus et desiderium probandi quae
vires essent novae, quam tum primum
tractabat, navi. Sedit animo experiri
115 mare, quod eo fatebatur esse periculos-
ius quo angustius.

5 · CELOX PERDITA

Neque periculum longe aberat; ventis
enim turgentibus et mari exasperato,
120 circa mediam noctem videre erat
celocem procul duo lumina e carchesio
protendentem. Tum scilicet actum de
illa esse et altis haustam vorticibus
existimabamus; momento enim
125 conspectum effugerat, neque nisi post
sex septimanas eius inditium aliquod ad
nos emanavit. Itaque periisse celocem
cunctis erat persuasum; meliora tamen
providerat Deus; nam se fluctibus
130 imparem sentiens mature oceanum
Virginium, cum quo iam nos luctabamur, devitans, in Angliam ad insulas
Sillinas revertit; unde postliminio,
Dracone comite ad sinum magnum,
135 nos ad insulas Antillas, ut dicemus, est
assecuta, Deo, cui minimorum cura est,
exiguae naviculae ut duce et custode
prospiciente.

---

104 ferr *ms* ferro *Dalrymple, Hughes* 109 Hybernicum *ms*
coecis *ms* 123 Celox perdita *in marg. sin.* 137 de duce *ms*

NAVIS FLUCTIBUS PERMISSA

eventus, -us, m. — outcome
ignarus, -a, -um, with Gen. — ignorant of
teter = taeter, -tra, -trum — abominable, gloomy, hideous
fetus = fetus, -a, -um, with abl. — teeming with, full of
illucescente die — 'at daybreak'
africus, -i — south-west wind
contrarius, -a, -um — opposed, blowing against
languidus, -a, -um — weak, mild
per multas ambages — 'making frequent tacks'
provehor, -vehi — to sail, advance
dies Martis — Tuesday
dies Mercurii — Wednesday
dies Iovis — Thursday
exiguus, -a, -um — small, little
varians, -antis — variable
profectus, -us — progress
dies Veneris — Friday
obtineo, 2 — to prevail
euronotus, -i — south-east wind
glaucus, -a, -um — bluish-grey
gravidus, -a, -um — laden, full, filled, thick
turbo, -inis, m. — whirling around, tempest
effundo, -fundere, -fusi, -fusum — here: to break forth
singulis momentis — 'with every motion'
ut involvendi videremur — 'that it seemed that we would be enveloped'
mitis, -e — soft, mild
lux Andreae apostolo sacro — 'the day sacred to the Apostle Andrew,' 'St. Andrew's Day'
promitto, 3 — to send forth, promise
lux, lucis, f. — here: day
terrificum in morem — in a terrifying manner
undique — from all sides
concresco, 3 — to grow, collect
intueor, 2 (dep.) — to look at attentively, gaze at
antequam — before
discindo, 3 — to split
opinio, -onis, f. — opinion, belief
opinionem faciebant — White distances himself from the superstitious view reported in this passage.
prodeo, -ire, -ii, itum — to come out, appear, go forward
acies, -ei, f. — line of battle
tempestas, -atis, f. storm, tempest
maleficus, -a, -um — evil-doing, mischievous
genius, -ii — spirit, genius

PISCIS SOLIS

inclinante die — 'towards evening'
navarchus, -i — captain
piscis Solis — sunfish
cursus solaris, -e — course of the sun
obnitor, 3 (dep.) with dat. — to strive against
horridus, -a, -um — dreadful, horrible
indicium, -ii — sign
fides, -ei — here: fulfilment
augurium, -ii — omen, prophecy
nocturna (hora), -ae — hour of the night
coecus = caecus, -a, -um — dark
atrox, -ocis — terrible, violent
depluit, -ere — to rain down
imber, -bris, m. — shower (of rain)
immanis, -e — enormous, immense
turbo, -inis, m. — whirling around, tempest
suscipio, -cipere, -cepi, -ceptum — to take up, raise
quantocyus — as quickly as possible
velum, -i — sail
contraho, 3 — to draw together, furl
neque id fieri tam expedite potuit quam acatium ...finderetur — 'this could not be done quickly enough to prevent the main sail...from being torn'
acatium = acatium velum — main sail
deorsum — downwards
aegre — with difficulty, scarcely

6 · NAVIS FLUCTIBUS PERMISSA

140 At vero nos eventus ignaros dolor et metus premebat, quem tetra nox frequentibus feta terroribus augebat. Illucescente die, cum africum haberemus contrarium, quia tamen 145 languidior erat, per multas ambages lente provehebamur. Ita Martis, Mercurii et Iovis dies, variantibus ventis, exiguo profectu abiere. Die Veneris, obtinente euronoto et glaucas 150 cogente nubes vento gravidas, tantus circa vesperam se turbo effudit ut momentis singulis involvendi fluctibus videremur. Neque mitiora promittebat lux insequens Andreae apostolo sacra. 155 Nubes terrificum in morem undique concrescentes terrori erant intuentibus antequam discinderentur; et opinionem faciebant prodiisse adversum nos in aciem omnes spiritus tempestatum 160 maleficos et malos genios omnes Marilandiae.

7 · PISCIS SOLIS

Inclinante die, vidit navarchus piscem Solis cursui solari obnitentem, quod horridae tempestatis certissimum 165 indicium; neque fides abfuit augurio. Nam circa decimam nocturnam coeca nubes atrocem depluit imbrem. Hunc tam immanis turbo suscepit ut necesse 170 fuerit quantocyus ad vela contrahenda accurrere; neque id fieri tam expedite potuit quam acatium, seu velum maius, quo solo navigabamus, medium a summo deorsum finderetur. Eius pars 175 una in mare delata aegre recepta est.

142 navis fluctibus permissa *in marg. sin.* 141 praemebat *ms*
149 eurnoto *ms* 163 Piscis Solis *in marg. dext.*

VOTA ET PRECES CATHOLICORUM

fortissimi cuiusque — 'of even the bravest'
vector, -oris, m. — passenger
consterno, 1 — to frighten, alarm
procella, -ae — storm, tempest
praecipito, 1 — to cast headlong down, wreck
accendo, -cendere, -cendi, -censum — to kindle
votum, -i — vow
Immaculatae eiusdem Conceptionis — 'of her Immaculate Conception'. According to the Catholic faith, the Virgin Mary is the Immaculate Conception, i.e., she was conceived without original sin.
patronus, -i — patron saint
angelus tutelaris — guardian angel
ibidem — (in the same place,) of the same country
sacra exomologesi (abl.) — 'through the Sacrament of Penance' (confession of sins)
expio, 1 — to purify
clavus, -i — tiller, helm, rudder
moderamen, -inis, n. — means of guiding, control
navigium, -i — ship, vessel
fluctuo, 1 — to be tossed about
postea... quam, with subjunctive — but after
discus, -i — discus, quoit
aperio, -ire — to open up
occupo, 1 — to seize
oratio, -onis, f. — prayer
pro, with abl. — in proportion to, 'than'
minus tepide — 'in a less lukewarm way'
impendo, -pendere, -pendi, -pensum — to expend, lay out
tempus impendere — to spend time, devote time to
propositum, -i — purpose
barbarus, -i — foreigner, barbarian
honoro, 1 — to honor, glorify
Servator, -oris, m. — Savior
conatus, -us, m. — effort, undertaking
tenuis, -e — feeble
secundo, 1 — to favor, assist
dignor, 1 (dep.) — to consider worthy
dos, dotis, f. — gift
Immaculata Virgo Mater — Immaculate Virgin Mother (see note above on the Virgin Mary)
affulgeo, -ere, -fulsi, fulsum — to shine (upon)
intus — within, inside, to the inside, inwardly
mediocris, -e — moderate, ordinary; here: small
saevio, -ire, -ivi, itum — to rage

8 · VOTA ET PRECES CATHOLICORUM

Hic fortissimi cuiusque, sive vectoris sive nautae, est consternatus animus; fatebantur enim vidisse se celsas naves

180 minori procella praecipitatas. Accendit vero is turbo catholicorum preces et vota in honorem Beatissimae Virginis Matris et Immaculatae eiusdem Conceptionis, Sancti Ignatii patroni

185 Marilandiae, Sancti Michaelis et tutelarium omnium ibidem angelorum. Et quisque animum suum sacra exomologesi expiare contendebat; nam, clavi moderamine amisso, navigium

190 iam undis et ventis derelictum fluctuabat ut in aqua discus, dum Deus saluti viam aperiret. Initio, fateor, occupaverat me metus amittendae navis et vitae; postea vero quam tempus

195 aliquod orationi, minus pro more meo quotidiano tepide, impendissem atque Christo Domino, Beatissimae Virgini, Sancto Ignatio, et angelis Marilandiae exposuissem propositum huius intineris

200 esse, sanguinem Redemptoris nostri in salute barbarorum honorare, eidem Servatori regnum (si conatus tenues secundare dignetur) erigere, dotem alteram Immaculatae Virgini Matri

205 consecrare, et similia multa, affulsit intus in animo consolatio non mediocris et simul persuasio tam certa nos non ab hac procella tantum, sed ab omni alia itinere isto liberandos, ut

210 nullus apud me esse posset dubitandi locus. Dederam me orationi cum mare saeviret maxime, et (quod ad Dei unius

179 Vota et preces Catholicorum *in marg. dext.*
191 discas *ms* discus *Hughes*

vix dum — scarcely yet
finio, -ire, -ivi, -itum — to finish
finieram = finiveram
animadverto, 3 — to take notice of, perceive
scilicet — certainly, of course
induo, -ere, -dui, -dutum — (to clothe), provide with
habitus, -us, m. — attitude, disposition
perfundo, -fundere, -fudi, -fusum — to fill with
gaudium,, -ii — joy
admiratio, -onis, f. — wonder
propensus, -a, -um — inclined, well-disposed
amplius — 'more fully', 'more grandly'
persentio, -ire — to perceive distinctly, feel deeply
Reverentia Vestra — Your Reverence (formal address of the Father General of the Jesuits)
Redemptor -oris — Savior

gloriam cedat) vix dum eam finieram
cum sedisse animadvertebam

215 tempestatem. Id scilicet novo quodam
me induit habitu animi perfuditque
simul gaudio ingenti et admiratione,
cum propensam Dei in Marilandiae
populos voluntatem (ad quos

220 Reverentia Vestra nos misit) haud paulo
amplius persentirem. Dulcissima
Redemptoris nostri bonitas in aeternum
laudetur. Amen.

9 · REDDITA SALUS

REDDITA SALUS

defervesco, -fervescere, -ferbui — to cease to rage
placidus, -a, -um — quiet, gentle
assevero, 1 — to assert
incommodum -i — inconvenience, disadvantage
nomino, 1 — to mention, speak about
insedo, -ere, -sedi, -sessum — here: to be at (sea)
integer, -gra, -grum — complete, whole, entire
iter integrum - the entire (or actual) voyage
Antillae insulae — the Antilles, or West Indies (the cluster of islands between North and South America, separating the Caribbean from the Atlantic)
adnumero, 1 — to reckon in
hebdomadas, -adis (acc. plu. **hebdomadas**), f. — week
solummodo — only
tenuit — 'lasted'
expeditus, -a, -um — quick

225 Cum itaque deferbuisset iam mare,
reliqua trium mensium navigatio
placidissima fuit ut navarchus cum suis
iucundiorem se vidisse nunquam, aut
quietiorem asseveraverit; neque enim

230 unius horae passi sumus incommodum.
Cum vero tres menses nomino, non
dico nos tamdiu mare insedisse, sed iter
integrum et moras, quas in Antillis
insulis traximus, adnumero; navigatio

235 enim ipsa septem hebdomadas et duos
solummodo dies tenuit, idque censetur
iter expeditum.

10 · A TURCIS METUUNT

A TURCIS METUUNT

littus Hispaniae — the coast of Spain
lego, 3 — to traverse, coast along, sail along
admodum — completely, wholly
prosper(us), -era, -erum — favorable
vereor, 2 (dep.) — to be afraid, fear
Turcae, -arum — the Turks
obvius, -a, -um — in the way
se recipere — to withdraw
fortasse — perhaps
ieiunium, -ii — fast, abstinence
Isom — sawm (fasting required of Muslims during the month of Ramadan)
tempestas, -atis, f. — here: time, season

240 Ab eo igitur tempore quando littus
Hispaniae legebamus, neque adverso,
neque vento admodum prospero usi
sumus. Verebamur Turcas, nullos
tamen habuimus obvios; receperant
fortasse se ad solemne ieiunium, quod

245 iam Isom vocant, celebrandum; in illam
enim anni tempestatem incidebat.

227 Reddita salus *in marg. sin.*   239 A Turcis metuunt *in marg. dext.*

Fretum Herculaneum — the Strait of Gibraltar
Maderae, -arum — the Madeira Islands (far off the Moroccan coast on the Atlantic Ocean; the largest of them is called Madeira)
puppis, -is, f. — stern of a vessel
* **velum, -i** — sail
impleo, 2 — to fill
vagus, -a, -um — wandering, fickle, variable
auster, -stri — south
africus, -i — southwest
cursus, -us, m. — course
constanter — steadily
sedeo, 2 — to stay fixed
disto, -are — to be apart, be distant, be away
leuca, -ae — league (nautical measure of distance, about three and a half miles)
occidens, -ntis — west
conor, 1 — here: to try to come
interdum — sometimes, now and then
obviam, with dat. — towards, against
ad invicem — 'towards each other'
ultro citroque — 'back and forth'
mitto, 3 — here: to send messengers
percontor, 1 — to inquire, investigate
suspicor, 1 — to suspect
piratica, -ae — piracy; translate: pirates
expedio, -ire — to get things ready
* **navarchus, -i** — captain
stimulo, 1 — to incite, stir up
ultro — of one's own accord, gratuitously
aggredior, 3 (dep.) — to approach, attack
lacesso, 3 — to provoke, induce
sed...ratio — word order: **sed cum dominum habebat cui reddenda erat ratio**
rationem reddere — to render account, be accountable to
causam afferre — to give a (plausible) reason
conflictum difficilem habiturum fuisse — 'that he would have had a difficult confrontation'
coniectura assequor — 'I would guess', 'I would infer'
mercator, -oris, m. — merchant
Fortunatae, -arum — the Fortunate, or Canary Islands (off the coast of northwest Africa, on the Atlantic Ocean)
dissitus, -a, -um — scattered
tendo, 3 — to direct one's course, make towards

SINUS MAGNUS

insulae Fortunatae — the Canary Islands (off the coast of northwest Africa, on the Atlantic Ocean)
suscipio, -cipere, -cepi, -ceptum — to receive
suscepti fuimus = suscepti sumus. Though rarely, **fui** is sometimes used in place of **sum** in the perfect passive, even in classical Latin.
malacia, -ae — windless period, a calm at sea
15 diebus — 'for fifteen days' (abl. instead of acc.)
septimana, -ae — week
perduro, 1 — to last
deficio, -ficere — to fail
commeatus, -us, m. — provisions, food
nihilominus — nevertheless
spiro, 1 — to blow

Praetervectis autem fretum Herculeum
et Maderas, et ventis puppi vela
implentibus (qui non iam vagi sed ad
250 austrum et africum, qui noster erat
cursus, constanter sedent), apparuerunt
tres naves, quarum una nostram mole
superabat; distare autem videbantur ad
tres circiter leucas versus occidentem et
255 nobis obviam conari, interdum etiam
ad invicem ultro citroque mittere et
percontari. Cum suspicaremur esse
Turcarum piraticas, expediebamus
quaecumque ad pugnam erant
260 necessaria. Neque deerant ex nostris
qui navarchum imprudentius
stimularent ut eas ultro aggrederetur ac
lacesseret; sed dominum habebat cui,
cum reddenda erat ratio, probabilem se
265 posse pugnae causam afferre dubitabat.
Et quidem conflictum difficilem
habiturum fuisse existimo; quamquam
fortasse quantum ab illis nos, tantum
nos illi metuebant, et erant, ut
270 coniectura assequor, mercatores qui ad
Fortunatas non procul dissitas
tendebant, et vel non poterant nos
assequi, vel nolebant.

11 · SINUS MAGNUS

275   Hinc ad insulas Fortunatas delati,
sinu magno suscepti fuimus, in quo
nullus metus nisi a malaciis, quae
cum 15 diebus et tribus aliquando
septimanis perdurent, deficit navigantes
280 commeatus. Id vero raro et vix saeculo
uno semel aut iterum accidit; frequen-
tissime nihilominus trahendae sunt

258 pyraticas *ms*   **277** Sinus magnus *in marg. sin.*

navigatio, -ionis, f. — voyage
propitius, -a, -um — favorable
conficio, -ficere, -feci, -fectum — to pass through, travel
milliare (gen. plu. milliarium) Italicum — Italian mile. Perhaps
White means a Roman mile here, about 1620 yards.
seco, 1 — to cut through, traverse, pass over
lacteus, -a, -um — milky; here, 'foaming'
nusquam — nowhere
quandoque — at some time or other, occasionally

CUR HIC SINT VENTI ET PLUVIAE CERTAE?

White probably included this section in response to the keen
interest in meteorology which the Father General and recipient of
the report, Mutius Vitelleschi, had demonstrated by his treatise on
Aristotle's discussion of the topic (*In libros meteorologicorum
Aristotelis disputationes*, 1590).
forte — by chance
quis dixerit — 'one might say'
vicinia, -ae — vicinity, neighborhood
tropicus, -i — tropic (either of the two circles of the celestial
sphere, on each side of and parallel to the equator, which the sun
reaches at its greatest declination north or south)
intercurro, 3 — to run between, pass between
attraho, 3 — to draw, attract
meteora, -ororum — vapors
siccus, -a, um — dry
marinus, -a, -um — of the sea
salsedo, -inis, f. — saltiness
humidus, -a, -um — wet, moist
ratione — by reason of
genero, 1 — to produce
pluvia, -ae — rain
eveho, 3 — to carry up, draw
obliquus, -a, -um — oblique
cursus, -us, m. — course
perpetuo — uninterruptedly, constantly
cur...experti sumus — the use of the indicative in this indirect
question is obviously a mere oversight, as the other indirect
questions in the paragraph are correctly formed with the
subjunctive.
calor, -oris, m. — warmth, heat
copiosus, -a, -um — plentiful, abundant
mane — in the morning
saltem — at least
vehemens, -ntis — violent, furious
malacia, -ae — windless period, calm at sea
tropicus Capricorni — Tropic of Capricorn (the southern one of
the two tropics)
exsisto, 3 — to stand, appear
linea aequinoctialis — equinoctial line (the celestial equator)
meridionalis, -e — southern

morae, deficiente vento; qui, cum spirat, unus et idem semper est huic
285 nostrae navigationi propitius. In hoc sinu confecimus milliarium Italicorum tria milia, plenis velis mare secantes lacteum, nusquam impediente malacia, nisi quandoque circa meridiem una
290 hora.

12 · CUR HIC SINT VENTI ET PLUVIAE CERTAE

Haud facilem invenio rationem tam constantis venti nisi   forte id oriri quis dixerit ex vicinia solis inter duos
295 tropicos intercurrentis et vi sua attrahentis ex mari duo genera meteororum, siccum unum ex marina salsedine, alterum humidum ratione aquae: ex priori fit ventus, ex posteriori
300 generantur pluviae. Sol itaque utrumque ad se evehens causa est cur eundem cum sole obliquum semper cursum servent solemque perpetuo sequantur. Atque eadem potuit esse
305 ratio cur inter duos tropicos experti sumus ingentem simul calorem et copiosam pluviam, idque constanter mane, meridie, vespere, vel saltem ventos iis horis vehementiores. Hinc
310 etiam deduci potest ratio cur hoc tempore sinus a malaciis liber fuerit: nam sol in tropico Capricorni existens ultra lineam aequinoctialem, et ad eiusdem lineae extremam partem
315 meridionalem declinans (ut nobis accidit inter tertium decimum et septimum decimum gradum aequatoris

294 Cur hic sint venti et pluviae certae *in marg. sin.*
297 meteorum *ms*

declino, 1 — to turn, swerve
hibernus, -a, -um — of winter
aestivus, -a, -um — of summer
* gradus, -us, m. — degree
praesertim — especially, chiefly
tropicus Cancri — Tropic of Cancer (the northern tropic)
aqueus, -a, -um — of water, watery
perpendicularis, -e — perpendicular (at a right angle)

MORBI EX VINO

extollo, 3 — to praise, extol
coopero, 1 — to work together
solvo, 3 — here: to sail
eo tempore...quo constitueramus — 'at the time we had settled upon'. Originally the departure of the *Ark* and *Dove* had been scheduled for mid-August, but opponents of the enterprise caused a delay of several months.
scilicet — evidently, certainly
cis, with acc. — on this side of
vertex -icis, m. — head, crown of the head
intensus, -a, -um — intense
calor, -oris, m. — heat
annona, -ae — produce, grain, provisions
labes, labis, f. — blemish
conscendo, 3 — to go on board ship, embark
consuetus, -a, -um — accustomed, usual
nausea, -ae — nausea, sea-sickness
excipio, -cipere, -cepi, -ceptum — to except
festum Nativitatis Domini — feast of the Nativity of the Lord, Christmas
celeber, -bris, -bre — celebrated, festive
propino, 1 — to drink
intemperans, -ntis — unrestrained, intemperate
febris, -bris, f. — fever
lux, lucis, f. — here: day

positis, quando mensibus nostris hibernis calores sunt ibi quanti aestivis
320 mensibus in Europa), attrahit oblique ventum et pluviam ad lineam aequinoctialem; atque inde iis mensibus venti sunt certiores, et in hoc sinu praesertim et versus tropicum
325 Cancri; frequentiores autem sunt malaciae, cum aestivo tempore sol aequatorem transit ad nos attrahitque meteora salsa et aquea, non oblique sed fere perpendiculariter.

330 ## 13 · MORBI EX VINO

Hic autem non possum non extollere divinam bonitatem, quae diligentibus Deum facit ut omnia cooperentur in bonum. Si enim, nulla
335 iniecta mora, licuisset eo tempore solvere quo constitueramus, mensis scilicet Augusti vigesimo, sole cis aequatorem verticem feriente, intensissimi calores non solum annonae
340 labem, sed plerisque omnibus morbos mortemque attulissent. Mora saluti fuit; nam hieme conscendentes huius-modi incommodis caruimus; et, si consuetas navigantibus nauseas
345 excipias, nemo morbo aliquo tentatus est usque ad festum Nativitatis Domini. Is dies ut celebrior esset, propinatum est vinum, quo qui usi sunt intemperantius, febri correpti sunt proxima luce numero
350 triginta, et ex iis, non ita multo post, mortui sunt circiter duodecim; inter

---

319 hybernis *ms* **328** metiora *ms* **350** Morbi ex vino *in marg. sin.* **342** hyeme *ms*

circiter — about
desiderium, -ii — grief (for the loss of a person)
Nicolaus Farfaxius, Jacobus Barefote — the names of both participants in the expedition, Nicholas Fairfax and James Barefoot, are latinized here, as was the custom in manydocuments at the time. Nicholas Fairfax is named as one of the gentlemen investors in a document of 1635. James Barefoot is not mentioned in this list and may have been among the indentured servants. Their passage was paid for by one of the gentlemen investors, for whom they then had to work for four or five years. After that they were intitled to some land and supplies to start out as independent landowners.

PISCES VOLANTES. AVES TROPICAE

curiosus, -a, -um — curious
aequor, -oris, n. — (flat surface of the) sea
pinna, -ae — wing
seco, 1 — to cut, pass through
passer, -eris, m. — sparling (the European smelt, a small food fish resembling the trout and living along the coast, or in lakes)
splanula, -ae — smelt (bigger than the type of smelt referred to above)
pergratus, -a, -um — very pleasant
centeni, -ae, -a — a hundred together
gregatim — in crowds
libro, 1 — to hurl, rise into the air
delphinus, -i — dolphin
* deficio, -ficere — to fail
remigium, -ii — oars
impetus, us, m. — impulse, leap
iugerum, -i; gen. plur. iugerum — translate: acre
spatium, -ii — space
verbero, 1 — to beat, strike
exsiccatus, -a, -um — dried
immergo, 3 — to plunge into, immerse
videre erat = vidimus
pendulus, -a, -um — hanging, hovering
cum...adaequent — this is best translated as a main clause: 'they equal...'
falco, -onis, m. — falcon
duabus...conspicuae — supply sunt
praelongus, -a, -um — very long
albeo, 2 — to be white
pluma, -ae — feather
cauda, -ae — tail
insideo, 2 — to remain
quandoque — sometimes
se sustentare — to rest
ut aliorum litteris nota — 'as known from the letters of others'
omitto, 3 — to omit

quos duo catholici magnum sui apud omnes desiderium reliquerunt Nicolaus Farfaxius et Iacobus Barefote.

355   14 · PISCES VOLANTES. AVES TROPICAE

    Inter navigandum, multa occurrebant curiosa: in primis pisces qui modo aequor, modo aera sublime pinnis secabant, passerum magnitudine vel
360 maiorum splanularum, quas valde etiam gustu pergrato referunt. Centeni gregatim se in aere librant, delphinos cum fugiunt insequentes. Eorum aliqui, deficiente pinnarum remigio, in
365 nostram navem deciderunt; nam uno impetu non amplius quam duorum vel trium iugerum spatium pervolant; tum pinnas aerem verberando exsiccatas aquis rursus immergunt et se iterum
370 caelo committunt. Cum ab aequatore uno et viginti gradibus et aliquot minutis abessemus, ubi tropicus incipit, videre erat aves quas a loco tropicas vocant in aere pendulas. Illae cum
375 falconem mole adaequent, duabus praelongis et albentibus plumis in cauda conspicuae, incertum est an aeri perpetuo insideant, an quandoque aquis se sustentent. Cetera ut aliorum
380 litteris nota omitto.

---

356 post conspectum piscem Solis qui cursui solis obnititur, et est index tempestatum, postque tempestatem non unam *altera manus inseruit* volantes *altera manus inseruit*   Pisces volantes *in marg. sin.*   **374** Aves tropicae *in marg.sin.*   **375** adequent *ms* **379** caetera *ms*

BONAVISTA SALE ET CAPREIS ABUNDAT

insulae Fortunatae — the Canary Islands (off the coast of northwest Africa, in the Atlantic Ocean)
Leonardus Calvert — Leonard Calvert, the younger brother of Cecilius Calvert, Lord Baltimore, was the leader of the expedition and the first governor of Maryland.
praefectus, -i — governor, commander
classis, -is — fleet
agito, 1 — to discuss, consider
merx, mercis, f. — merchandise, goods
comparo, 1 — to provide, to buy
quas merces...onerandae — 'which goods should be loaded on the ship for her return, and where they were to be had'
Baron de Baltimor — though generally, and also properly, addressed 'Lord Baltimore', Cecilius Calvert's father George had actually received the title of 'Baron of Baltimore' for his outstanding service as an official of the English Crown.
sumptus, -us, m. — cost, expense
caveo, 2, with dat. — to take care of
princeps, -cipis — leader, initiator
incumbo, 3, with dat. — to lie upon
nostras, -atis — of our country; here: countryman
plantatio, -onis, f. — plantation, settlement
infensus, -a, -um — hostile
sunt...infensi — the Virginians would, of course, have preferred to make economic use of the area granted to Lord Baltimore themselves; in addition, they shared the resentment against Roman Catholics exhibited by Protestants in England. Surprisingly enough, however, the governor of Virginia assisted the Maryland colonists for his own reasons (see below, chapter 24).
insula Sancti Christophori — St. Christopher, known as St. Kitts today (island among the West Indies, or Antilles)
tendo, 3 — to tend, make towards
adhibeo, 2 — to bring to bear, employ
vereor, 2 (dep.) — to fear
serus, -a, -um — late
praevenio, -ire — to come before
prora, -ae — bow of a ship, ship
obverto, 3 — to turn towards
potior, -iri, -itus sum, (dep.) with gen. — here: to reach
auster, -stri — south
littus (-oris, n.) Africanum — the African coast
gradibus 14 ab aequatore — 14 degrees from the equator
statio, -onis, f. — post, station
Hollandi, -orum — the Dutch
sal, salis, m. — salt
conquiro, 3 — to get together, collect
Groenlandia, -ae — Greenland
condio, -ire — to pickle, preserve
caprea, -ae — goat
alioqui — otherwise, in other respects
habitator, -oris, m. — inhabitant
Lusitani, -orum — the Portuguese
exilio pellere — to exile, to banish into exile
vitam trahunt — '(they) drag out their lives'
milliare, -is, n. — mile
suggestio, -onis, f. — suggestion
commeatus, -us, m. — provisions, food
deficio, -ficere — here: to run out
circuitus, -us, m. — roundabout way
deflecto, -flectere, -flexi, flectum — to turn away
Barbados — Barbados (another island of the West Indies, or Antilles)

15 • BONVISTA SALE ET CAPREIS ABUNDAT

Cum insulas Fortunatas essemus praetervecti, Dominus Leonardus Calvert praefectus classis agitare coepit
385 quas merces et unde comparare posset navi reduci onerandae quo fratris sui Baronis de Baltimor sumptibus caveret; illi enim ut totius navigationis principi onus integrum incumbebat. In
390 Virginia a nostratibus nihil commodi sperabatur, sunt enim huic novae plantationi infensi. Itaque ad insulam Sancti Christophori tendebamus cum, consilio adhibito, verentes ne ea anni
395 sera tempestate alii nos praevenissent, proras obvertimus ad austrum, ut Bonavistae potiremur; quae insula Angolae opposita in littore Africano, gradibus 14 ab aequatore, statio est
400 Hollandorum salem conquirentium, quem deinde vel domum, vel ad piscem in Groenlandia condiendum conferunt. Copia salis atque etiam caprearum, quarum insula ferax est, eo nos
405 invitabat; nam alioqui habitatore nullo utitur. Pauci tantum Lusitani, exilio propter scelera pulsi, vitam ut possunt trahunt. Vix ducenta milliaria confeceramus cum, mutatis iterum
410 quorundam suggestione consiliis ne commeatus in tanto circuitu nos deficeret, deflectimus ad Barbados.

---

398 Bonavista sale et capreis abundat *in marg. dext.*
400 Holandorum *ms* **402** Groelandia *ms*
403 caprarum *ms* **412** Barbados *in marg. dext.*

BARBADOS. MERCES CARAE

ea = Barbados
Carebes insulae, Antillae insulae — the Caribbean Islands, or Antilles (West Indies)
infimus, -a, -um — lowest, last
* **gradus, -us**, m. — degree
distans, -ntis — distant
arcus, -us, m. — bow, arch
sinus Mexicanus — the Gulf of Mexico
tractus, -us, m. — trail, line
protendo, 3 — to stretch
granarium, -ii — granary
Ianuarius, -ii — January
appello, -pellere, -puli, -pulsum — to reach
commoditas, -atis, f. — here: article of trade
Angli, -orum — the English
ab...consanguineo gubernatore — 'from the governor, who was a brother of a member of the expedition'. The governor of Barbados was a brother of Hierom Hawley, one of Leonard Calvert's gentleman associates and later one of three councillors assisting Calvert in administering the Maryland colony. Hawley's brother was absent at the time, however, which may account for the disappointing reception.
conspiratio, -onis, f. — conspiracy, plot
modius, -ii — grain-measure; bushel
triticum -i — here: wheat. Wheat had to be procured above all to be sown in Maryland and provide food during the following year. It was not available in England.
veneo, venire, with abl. — to be sold for, to go on sale
qui medio floreno Belgico veniebat — 'which used to be sold for half a Belgian florin'
quintupla proportione — 'for five times the amount'
duobus florenis cum dimidio — 'for two and a half florins'
vendo, 3 — to sell
nefrens, -ndis, m. — suckling pig
licito, 1, with abl. — to offer at (a certain price)
pullus Indicus — turkey
altilis, is — fowl
bovina, -ae — beef
vervecina, -ae — mutton
panis Indicus — Indian bread (corn-bread)
radix, -icis, f. — root
plaustrum -i — cart
gratis — without recompense, for nothing

DIVINA PROVIDENTIA

mitigo, 1 — to make mild, soothe, mitigate
exterus, -a, -um — foreign
commercium, -ii — trade, commerce
* **porro** — further
contendo, 3 — to hasten, strive
casses, -ium, m. pl. — trap
praeda, -ae — prey
decido, -cidere, -cidi, -casurus — to fall
famulus, -i — servant, slave

16 • BARBADOS. MERCES CARAE

Est ea Carebum seu Antillarum
415 insularum infima, ab aequatore 13
tantum gradibus distans, ceterarumque
(quae in modum arcus ad usque sinum
Mexicanum longo tractu protenduntur)
granarium. Ad hanc ut appulimus
420 tertio Ianuarii, in spem venimus
multarum commoditatum ab incolis
Anglis et consanguineo gubernatore;
sed conspiratione facta modium tritici,
qui in insula medio floreno Belgico
425 veniebat, nobis non nisi quintupla
proportione, duobus florenis cum
dimidio, vendere decreverunt. Nefren-
dem unum quinquaginta florenis
licitabant; pullum Indicum viginti
430 quinque, caetera eius generis altilia
minora tribus florenis; bovinam seu
vervecinam nullam habebant; vivunt
enim pane Indico et potatis, quod
radicum genus tanta affluentia provenit
435 ut plaustra integra gratis auferre liceat.

17 • DIVINA PROVIDENTIA

Hominum acerbam severitatem
Divinae Providentiae consideratio
mitigavit. Intelleximus enim ad
440 insulam Bonavistae stare classem
Hispanicam quo exteros omnes salis
commercio prohiberent: illo si porro
contendissemus itinere constituto, in
casses praeda facti decidissemus.
445 Maiori interim periculo ad Barbados
erepti. Famuli per totam insulam in

424 Merces carae *in marg.sin.* 416 caeterarum *ms*
437 Divina Providentia *in marg. sin.* 441 Hispanicum *ms*

conspirarant = conspiraverant
scilicet — evidently
assero, -serere, -serui, -sertum — to add, claim
asserere in libertatem — to declare as free, to free
navi — ablative singular of **navis** can be **nave** or **navi**
appello, 3 — to reach, land
potior, 4 (dep.), with abl. — to get possession of, obtain
tento, 1 — to test, attempt
patefacio, -facere, -feci, factum — to disclose, reveal
praecipuus, -i — ringleader
littori applicare — to land
destinatus, -a, -um — determined, designated
reperio, reperire, repperi, repertum — to find, discover
quo, with subjunctive — so that through this (introduces a purpose clause)
obvio, 1 — to oppose

CALORES IMMENSI. LECTI. GOSSIPIUM

mirandus, -a, -um — wonderful
libet, libere — it pleases, is agreeable
* **milliare, -is, n.** — mile
disto, 1 — to be distant
calor, -oris, m. — heat
hibernus, -a, -um — of winter
linea, -orum — linen clothes
* **immergo, 3** — to immerse
messis, -is, f. — harvest
appello, -pellere, -puli, -pulsum — to reach, land
aestus, -us, m. — heat
tempero, 1 — to temper, mitigate
stragulum, -i — covering, carpet, cloth
vestis, -is, f. — carpet, tapestry
gossipium, -ii — cotton
affabre — skillfully
texo, texere, texui, textum — to weave, twine together
hac — refers to **vestis**
quiesco, 3 — to rest, sleep
funis, is, m. — rope
appensus, -a, -um — hung, hanging
hinc inde — on this side and on that side, on both ends from each side
palus, -i — pole, post
funibus...palos — 'after it has been hung by ropes from each side'
dormio, 4 — to sleep
de die — at daytime
iterum — on the other hand
merx, mercis, f. — article of trade, merchandise
praecipuus, -a, -um — chief, main
frumentum, -i — grain, corn
gossipium, -ii — cotton

necem dominorum conspirarant; tum scilicet in libertatem asserti navi, quae prima appelleret, potiri statuerunt et

450 tentare maria. Coniuratione patefacta per quendam, quem facti atrocitas deterrebat, supplicium unius ex praecipuis et insulae securitati et nobis saluti fuit; nostra enim navis, ut quae

455 prima littori applicuit, praedae destinata fuerat, et eo ipso die quo appulimus octingentos in armis reperimus quo recentissimo sceleri obviarent.

460 ## 18 · CALORES IMMENSI. LECTI. GOSSIPIUM

Miranda quaedam narrare libet quae haec insula profert. Triginta milliaria continet longitudo, latitudo 15, gradibus 13 distat ab aequatore, calore

465 tanto ut hibernis mensibus incolae lineis vestiantur et aquis se saepius immergant. Messis tum erat cum appulimus. Nisi frequentes venti aestum temperarent, impossibilis esset

470 habitatio. Lecti sunt stragula vestis ex gossipio affabre texta; in hac, cum est quiescendi tempus, funibus appensa ad duos hinc inde palos dormiunt; de die iterum quocumque libet auferunt.

475 Merces praecipuae sunt frumentum et gossipium. Iucundum est videre modum et copiam pendentis ex arbore gossipii. Arbor ex qua nascitur maior non est oxyacantho (quam vulgus

461 Calores immensae *in marg. dext.* **461-2** miranda... profert *altera manus delevit et explevit verbis* Insula Barbadorum **477** Gossipium *in marg. dext.*

berberis, -is — barberry (a shrub with spines, yellow flowers, and red berries)
spina, -ae — thorn bush
nodus, -i — here: pod
iuglans, -glandis, f. — walnut
acutus, -a, -um — pointed
dissectus, -a, -um — divided
nix, nivis, f. — snow
candidus, -a, -um — (shining) white
pluma, -ae — feather
in speciem — in the shape (of)
convolutus, -a, -um — rolled together
fundo, 3 — to give abundantly, give forth
semen, -inis, n. — seed
vicia, -ae — vetch (a genus of plants, some species of which are used as fodder; common in Europe and naturalized in America)
aequalis, -e — equal, similar to
rota, -ae — wheel
expedio, -ire, -ivi, -itum — to disentangle, separate
condo, 3 — to store, put away
saccus, -i — sack, bag
adservo, 1 — to preserve

INGENS BRASSICA

brassica, -ae — cabbage; here: cabbage tree
caulis, is, m. — stalk (of a plant, esp. cabbage)
crudus, -a, -um — raw
elixus, -a, -um — boiled
ulna, -ae — measurement of length; here: foot
mensura, -ae — measure, amount
deliciae, -arum, f.pl. — here: delicacies
admisceo, -ere, -miscui, -mixtum — to mix with
piper, piperis, n. — pepper
sapor, -oris, m. — taste, flavor
carduus Hispanicus — Spanish thistle (artichoke)
truncus, -i — trunk (of a tree)
adaequo, 1 — to come near to, equal
legumen, -inis, n. — leguminous plant
non amplius unam — 'no more than one'
videre est, with acc. — 'one can see'
sapo, -onis, f. — soap tree
procerus, -era, -erum — tall, long
granum, -i — seed
nux (genit. nucis) avellana — hazelnut
excedo, -cedere, -cessi, cessum — to exceed
pinguis, -e — oily, rich
tunica, -ae — covering
sapo, -onis, f. — soap
instar, n. — corresponding to, like
purgo, 1 — to clean, cleanse
detergo, 3 — to cleanse
linum, -i — linen
inimicus, -a, -um — adverse, detrimental, injurious
mando, 1 — to commit, plant

480 berberin vocat), quamquam arbori
quam spinae similior. Haec nodum fert
magnitudine iuglandis, forma acutiori,
qui in quatuor partes dissectus
gossipium nive candidius et pluma
485 mollius in speciem nucis convolutum
fundit. Gossipio sex parva semina
insident viciae aequalia, quod tempore
suo collectum et rota quadam a semine
expeditum condunt in saccos et
490 adservant.

19 • INGENS BRASSICA

Brassicae genus admirandum est,
quae cum caulem habeat in centum et
octoginta pedum altitudinem
495 excrescentem, vel cruda editur vel elixa.
Caulis ipse ad unius ulnae mensuram
sub fructu habetur in deliciis; crudus
admixto pipere sapore carduum
Hispanicum superat, et iuglandi
500 nudatae propior. Ingens caulis arboris
bene magnae truncum adaequans,
neque tamen arbor sed legumen,
brassicam fert non amplius unam.
Ibidem videre est arborem satis
505 proceram quam saponem vocant.
Grana saponis nucem avellanam non
excedunt magnitudine; horum pinguis
tunica; saponis instar, purgat et detergit,
quamquam, ut aiunt, lino tenuiori
510 inimica. Ex his granis multa mecum
ablata in Marilandiam mandavi terrae
futurarum arborum semina.

---

494 Ingens brassica *in marg. sin.*

PALMA CHRISTI. GNAVAR. PUPAES.
NUX PINEA

porosus, -a, -um — porous
legumen, -inis, n — leguminous plant (bean)
racemus, -i — cluster
subcinericius, -a -um — ashy
spina, -ae — thorn, prickle
niger, -gra, -grum — black, dark-colored
macula, -ae — spot, mark
inspergo, -ere, -spersi, -spersum — to sprinkle (on)
praestans, -ntis — excellent
oleum, -i — oil
malum aureum — orange
citrinum, -i — lemon
granatum, -i — pomegranate
calidus, -a, -um — warm, hot
ubertim — abundantly, copiously
provenio, -ire — to appear, come up
gnavar — guava (fruit)
citrus, -i — here: lemon
gustus, -us, m. — taste
referens, -ntis — recalling, resembling
cydonium — quince (an applelike fruit of a central Asiatic tree)
pupaes — papaw (papaya)
absimilis, -e — unlike
praedulcis, -e — very sweet
condio, -ire — to preserve (fruits etc.), 'give taste to'
cibus, -i — food
adhibeo, 2 — to bring up to, apply, use
praecello, 3 — to surpass, excel
alibi — elsewhere
gusto, 1 — to taste, partake of
nux Pinea — pineapple. Several earlier descriptions of the New World, such as Oviedo's famous *Historia general y natural de las Indias* (1535-57), also contained enthusiastic praise for the pineapple.
viror, -oris, m. — green (color)
eiusdem nominis nuces — i.e., pine cones
moles, -is, f. — mass
adaequo, 1 — to equal
admodum — wholly, quite
operosus, -a, -um — elaborate
distinctus, -a, -um — separate, destinct
loculamentum, -i — small division, cell
modulus, -i — a little measure, little part or division
nucleus, -i — kernel
involutus, -a, -um — rolled up (in), enveloped by
tenellus, -a, -um — thin
membranula, -ae — skin, membrane
acinus, -i — seed (of a fruit)
deorsum — downwards
palatum, -i — palate, taste
adrideo, 2 — to please
mereor, 2 (dep.) — to deserve
aromaticus, -a, -um — aromatic

20 • PALMA CHRISTI. GNAVAR. PUPAES. NUX PINEA

Inter arbores etiam numerant
515 palmam Christi; quamquam truncum
illa habeat porosum et legumini
similem, racemum fert ingentem
seminum coloris subcinericii, spinis
armatum et nigris maculis inspersum.
520 Ex his praestans oleum exprimitur.
Mala aurea, citrina, granata, nuces
etiam, quas Hispani cocos vocant,
ceterique calidarum regionum fructus
ubertim proveniunt.

Est et fructus qui gnavar dicitur,
coloris aurei, forma citri minoris, gustu
tamen referens cydonium. Pupaes
colore est et forma non absimili, sed
praedulcis cum sit condiendis tantum
530 cibis adhibetur.

Praecellit autem ceteris, quos alibi
terrarum gustavi fructus, nux Pinea.
Est ea coloris aurei virore mixta
gratissimo, tres vel quattuor eiusdem
535 nominis nuces Europaeas mole
adaequans, figura non admodum
dissimili, sed operosiore, non tot
distincta loculamentis et modulis, qui
ignem adhibiti nucleum reddant, sed
540 mollis et tenella involuta membranula,
gustui iucundissima, nullo aspera acino,
sed a summo deorsum aequaliter palato
arridens; neque deest, quam meretur,
corona; haud dubio enim regina
545 fructuum appellari potest. Gustum
habet aromaticum et quantum

516 Palma Christi *in marg. sin.* 523 caeterique *ms*
525 Gnavar *in marg. sin.* 527 Pupaes *in mag. sin.*
531 caeteris *ms* 533 nux Pinea *in margine dext.*
534 quatuor *ms*

coniectura assequor — 'I can guess', 'I would say'
fraga, -orum, n. pl. — strawberries
saccarum, -i — sugar
mistus = mixtus, -a, -um — mixed
referens, -ntis — recalling, resembling
sanitas, -atis, f. — health
consentio, -ire — to agree with
licet, with subjunctive — although
exedo, -edere or **-esse** — to eat up, destroy
hominem tamen, si qua res alia, quam maxime corroboret — 'it nonetheless strengthens man more than anything else'
praecelsus, -a, -um — very high
radix, -icis, f. — root
carduus Hispanicus, -i — Spanish thistle, artichoke
prominens, -ntis — projecting
Paternitas Vestra — Your Paternity (formal address of the Father General of the Jesuits)
pro, with abl. — here: according to
dignitas, -atis, f. — merit, excellence

SANCTA LUCIA. MATALINA.
INSULAE ANTILLAE SIVE CAREBUM

Ianuarius, -ii — January
anchoram subducere — to pull up the anchor, 'weigh anchor'
linter, -tris, f. — boat, skiff
vereor, -eri, veritus sum — to fear, be afraid
pepo, -onis — pepo, (a kind of) melon
cucurbita, -ae — gourd
platanus, -i, f. — plane tree
psittacus, -i — parrot
de longe — from afar
ostento, 1 — to show, offer
commuto, 1 — to exchange, barter
efferus, -a, -um — wild, savage
procerus, -a, -um — tall
obesus, -a, -um — fat, plump
pigmentum, -i — paint, pigment
niteo, 2 — to shine, be bright
carnium humanarum avidus — hungry for human flesh, 'practicing cannibalism'
interpres, -pretis, m. — interpreter
pridem — long ago
absumo, -sumere, -sumpsi, -sumptum — to consume
lucus, -i — grove, wood
planities, -ei, f. — plain
pervius, -a, -um — passable, accessible
aplustrum, -i — stern of a ship
propono, -ponere, -posui, -positum — to propose
album, -i — white flag
commercium, -ii — trade, commerce
aversor, 1 (dep.) — to turn away form, avoid

coniectura assequor fraga vino saccaroque mista referentem. Sanitati conservandae plurimum confert,
550 corporum constitutioni tam apte consentiens ut licet ferrum exedat, hominem tamen, si qua res alia, quam maxime corroboret; neque praecelsa hanc quaeras in arbore, sed unam una
555 ex radice quasi cardui Hispanici prominentem. Optabam me nucem unam Paternitati Vestrae cum hisce litteris tradere potuisse in manus; nihil enim illam praeter ipsam pro dignitate
560 potest describere.

21 · SANCTA LUCIA. MATALINA. INSULAE ANTILLAE SIVE CAREBUM

Vigesimo quarto Ianuarii de nocte subductis anchoris et circa meridiem sequentis diei, relicta ad laevam insula
565 Sanctae Luciae, sub vesperam tenuimus Matalinam. Hic duo lintres nudorum hominum, molem nostrae navis veriti, pepones, cucurbitas, fructus platani et psittacos, de longe ostentabant
570 commutandos. Gens effera, procera, obesa, pigmentis purpureis nitens, ignara numinis, carnium humanarum avida et quae Anglorum interpretes aliquot pridem absumpserat, regionem
575 incolit in primis fertilem, sed quae tota lucus sit, nulla planitie pervia. Aplustro albo in signum pacis proposito, eos qui se a longe ostentabant invitavimus ad commercia, sed, indicium aversati,

555 cardu *ms* 562 Sancta Lucia *in marg. dext.* 563 subductus *ms* 565 Matalina *in marg. dext.* 567 In insulis Antillae sive Carebum reperti obvii *altera manus addidit in marg. sup.* 572 Insulae Antillae sive Carebum *in marg. sin.*

insigne, -is, n. — mark, token
consuetus, -a, -um — accustomed, usual
insignia consueta — 'the usual colors', 'signs indicating our nationality', 'our national colors'
-nam — indicates question; not to be translated
resumo, -sumere, -sumpsi, -sumptum — to take again
accessere = accesserunt
tintinnabulum, -i — bell
cultellus, -i — little knife
praepotens, -ntis — very powerful
subsisto, 3 — to stay, remain
sequenti — ablative singular of **sequens, -ntis**
derelinquo, -linquere, -liqui, -lictum — to forsake, desert, abandon
miseratio, -onis, f. — pity, compassion
increbresco, -crebrescere, -crebui — to become strong, prevail, increase
Gallus, -i — French(man)
naufragus, -a, -um — shipwrecked
frons, frontis, f. — forehead
inusitatus, -a, -um — unusual, uncommon
splendor, -oris, m. — brilliance, brightness, splendor
insideo, 2 — to sit on
pruna, -ae — glowing coal
candela, -ae —candle
Carbuncula, -ae — the 'Carbuncle'
penes, with acc. — in the power of, belonging to
fides...auctorem — let proof of this matter belong to the author, 'let the originator of this story answer for its truth'

GUADALUPAE. MONSERRATE. MOEVIS. SANCTI CHRISTOPHORI

illucesco, 3 — to dawn, become light
Carebes insulae — the Caribbean Islands (islands in the Caribbean Sea). In White's report the terms 'Antilles' and 'Caribbean Islands' are used interchangeably (cf. chapter 21), but strictly speaking the Antilles are only part of the Caribbean Islands.
attingo, -tingere, -tigi, -tactum — to reach
quam asperorum... fecit cognomen — 'which is named after Guadalupe in Spain because of the similarity created by its rough mountains'
confido, 3 — to trust, be assured
tutela, -ae — protection
meridies, -ei, m. — midday, noon
Monserrate, -is — Montserrat, another Caribbean Island
lembus, -i — cutter (a small vessel)
Gallicus, -a, -um — French
Hispani, -orum — the Spanish
classis, -is, f. — fleet
tutus, -a, -um — safe
Hibernus, -a, -um — Irish
catholicus, -a, -um — (Roman) Catholic
professio, -onis, f. — declaration, profession
Moevium — acc. of **Moevis** (the Caribbean island Nevis)
pestilens, -ntis — unhealthy, fatal
febris, -is, f. — fever
infamis, -e — infamous
absumo, -sumere, -sumpsi, -sumptum — to consume, spend
vela fecimus — 'we set sail'

580 insignia consueta proposuerunt. Cum his ostensis quinam essemus intellexissent, animis resumptis accessere propius, sed paucis tantum tintinnabulis et cultellis acceptis, 585 praepotenti navi non nimium fidentes, celocem adeunt, promittentes se, si subsistere decerneremus, sequenti die meliores merces allaturos. Capiet olim aliquem, uti spero, derelicti huius 590 populi miseratio. Apud nautas increbuit rumor (ortus a Gallis quibusdam naufragis) reperiri in hac insula animal, cuius fronti lapis inusitati splendoris insidet, prunae vel candelae ardenti 595 similis. Huic animali Carbunculae nomen indiderunt. Rei fides sit penes auctorem.

22 • GUADALUPAE. MONSERRATE. MOEVIS. SANCTI CHRISTOPHORI

Die proximo illucescente, alteram 600 Carebum insularum attigimus, quam asperorum montium similitudo Hispanicae Guadalupae fecit cognomen, estque, uti confido, sub tutela eiusdem Sanctissimae Virginis Matris. Inde 605 Monserratem tenuimus circa meridiem, ubi ex lembo Gallico intelleximus nondum nos ab Hispanorum classe tutos esse. Habet Monserrate incolas Hibernos pulsos ab Anglis Virginia ob 610 fidei catholicae professionem. Tum ad Moevium pestilenti aere et febribus infamem. Uno die absumpto, vela

595 Carbuncae *ms* 597 authorem *ms* 602 Guadalupae *in marg. sin.* 609 Hybernos *ms* 611 Moevis *in marg. dext.*

Sancti Christophori — St. Christopher, known as St. Kitts today (a Caribbean island)
subsisto, -sistere, -stiti — to stop, stay, remain
gubernator, -oris, m. — governor
capitaneus, -i — captain
amice — in a friendly manner
benigne — kindly, generously
praefectus, -i — governor

MONS SULPHUREUS. PLANTA VIRGO. LOCUSTA ARBOR ET FRUCTUS

viso, 3 — to look at, see
reperio, -perire, repperi, repertum — to find, discover
* praefectus, -i — governor
sulphureus, -a, -um — of sulphur
mons sulphureus — 'sulphur mountain'; actually a 'mountain of brimstone'
admiror, 1 (dep.) — to wonder at, admire
planta Virgo — virgin plant
digitus, -i — finger
contactus, -us, m. — contact, touch
confestim — immediately
marcesco, 3 — to begin to droop
concido, 3 — to fall down, perish
revivisco, 3 — to come to life again, revive
assurgo, 3 — to rise up, stand up
marcescat...concidat...assurgat — translate as if these verbs were in the indicative
Locusta arbor — locust tree
quam suspitio est — 'which is supposed to'
victus, -us, m. — nourishment
Joannis Baptista — St. John the Baptist
ulmus, -i, f. — elm
adaequo, 1 — to equal
apis, -is — bee
libens, -ntis — willing, with pleasure
favus, -i — honeycomb
implico, 1 — to enfold, entwine
mel, mellis, n. — honey
si nomen silvestris demas — 'if you took away the term "wild"' (i.e., the honey is 'wild' in name only)
sapor, -oris, m. — taste, flavor
cortex, corticis, m. — bark, rind, shell
faba, -ae — broad bean
siliqua, -ae — pod
par, paris — equal, like
medulla, -ae — marrow, flesh
mollis, -e — here: supple
tenax, -acis — firm
gustus, -us, m. — taste
farina, -ae — meal, flour
mixtus, -a, -um — mixed
semen, seminis, n. — seed
grandiusculus, -a, -um — rather large
castaneus, -a, -um — of a chestnut
insero, 3 — to introduce, plant
asporto, 1 — to carry off

fecimus ad Sancti Christophori, ubi decem dies substitimus a gubernatore 615 Anglo et capitaneis duobus catholicis amice invitati; me in primis benigne accepit coloniae Gallicae in eadem insula praefectus.

23 · MONS SULPHUREUS. PLANTA VIRGO. LOCUSTA ARBOR ET FRUCTUS

620 Quaecumque apud Barbados rara visuntur hic etiam repperi, et praeterea non procul a praefecti sede montem sulphureum, et, quod admireris magis, plantam Virginem, sic dictam, quod 625 minimo digiti contactu confestim marcescat et concidat, quanquam data mora reviviscens iterum assurgat. Placuit mihi in primis Locusta arbor, quam suspitio est praebuisse victum 630 Sancto Joanni Baptistae; ulmum adaequat altitudine, apibus tam grata ut libentissime illi favos suos implicent; mel, si nomen silvestris demas, neque colore, neque sapore a purissimo quod 635 gustavi melle differt. Fructus etiam locustae nomen retinens in duriori cortice sex fabarum siliquis pari, medullam continet mollem, sed tenacem, gustu farinae similem melle 640 mixtae; semina fert grandiuscula quattuor vel quinque coloris castanei. Horum aliqua terrae inserenda asportavi.

614 Sancti Christophori *in marg. dext.* substituimus *ms* **619** Mons sulphureus *in marg. dext.* Planta Virgo *in marg. dext.* **621** reperere deinde *altera manus addidit in marg. sin.* **628** Placuit...primis *altera manus delevit;* ibidem *altera manus inseruit* Locusta arbor *in marg. dext.* **641** quatuor *ms*

CAPUT CONSOLATIONIS IN VIRGINIA

* solvo, 3 — to sail
hic — here: hereupon (or: from this place)
teneo, 2 — here: to reach
Februarius, -ii — February
machinor, 1 (dep.) — to contrive, devise
plantatio, -onis, f. — plantation, settlement
* admodum — completely
quaestor, -oris, m. — treasurer
Anglia, -ae — England
valuere = valuerunt
placo, 1 — to reconcile, appease
porro — here: in the future
ea quae... usui futura erant — 'things which would be useful'
impetro, 1 — to get, obtain
fiscus, -i — treasury
magnam vim pecuniae sibi debitae — 'a large sum of money due to him'
regius, a, -um — royal
recupero, 1 — to regain, recover
sperabat...recuperaturum — this explains at least in part why Sir John Harvey, the governor of Virginia, acted so graciously towards Lord Baltimore's expedition, while most Virginians resented the new settlement, which destroyed their economic monopoly in the Chesapeake. The episode may also have added to the Virginians' discontent with their governor, whom they soon replaced by a man of their choice. The king, however, countered this act of insubordination by reinstating Harvey with increased authority, a development which was, of course, advantageous for the colonists in Maryland.
spargo, spargere, sparsi, sparsum — to spread, circulate
nuncio = nuntio, 1 — to announce, give notice
advento, 1 — to approach, come near
Hispani, -orum — the Spanish
redigo, -igere, -egi, -actum — to bring (to a condition)
indigena, -ae — native
experti sumus — 'we found to be true'
ortus, -us, m. — origin

SINUS CHESOPEACH. PATOMEACH FLUVIUS, SIVE SANCTI GREGORII. PROMONTORIUM EIUSDEM SANCTI MICHAELIS

benignus, -a, -um — kind, friendly, generous
tractatio, -onis, f. — handling, treatment
Martius, -ii — (the month of) March
vela facere — to set sail
sinus, -us, m. — bay, gulf
invehor, -vehi, -vectus sum — to sail into, enter
aquilo, -onis, m. — north
deflecto, -flectere, -flexi, -flectum — to turn
fluvius, -ii — river
potior, -iri, potitus sum (dep.) — here: to reach
sinus Chesopeach — Chesapeake Bay
leuca, -ae — league (nautical measure of distance, about three and a half miles)
placidus, -a, -um — quiet, still, gentle

24 • CAPUT CONSOLATIONIS IN VIRGINIA

645   Ac tandem hic solventes, caput quod vocant Consolationis in Virginia tenuimus 27 Februarii, pleni metu ne quid mali nobis machinarentur Angli incolae, quibus nostra plantatio ingrata
670 admodum erat. Litterae tamen, quas a rege et a summo Angliae quaestore ad earum regionum praefectum ferebamus, valuere ad placandos animos, et ea quae nobis porro usui
675 futura erant impetranda. Sperabat enim praefectus Virginiae hac benevolentia erga nos facilius regio e fisco magnam vim pecuniae sibi debitae recuperaturum. Sparsum tantum
680 rumorem nunciabant adventare sex naves quae omnia sub Hispanorum potestatem redigerent; indigenas ea propter omnes in armis esse; quod verum postea experti sumus. Rumor
685 tamen, vereor, ab Anglis ortum habuit.

25 • SINUS CHESOPEACH. PATOMEACH FLUVIUS SIVE SANCTI GREGORII. PROMONTORIUM EIUSDEM SANCTI MICHAELIS

    Post octo vel novem dierum benignam tractationem, tertio Martii vela facientes et in sinum Chesopeach
690 invecti, cursum ad aquilonem defleximus ut fluvio Patomeach potiremur. Sinus Chesopeach latus decem leucas placide inter littora

---

647 Caput Consolationis in Virginia *in marg. sin.*
688 Sinus Chesopeach *in marg. sin.*

profundus, -a, -um — deep
orgyia (-ya), ae — fathom (ca. 6 feet)
cum favet annus — 'when it is the right time of the year'
scateo, 2 — to teem, abound
fluvius Patomeach —Potomac River
indo, -dere, -didi, -ditum — to give, confer
optatus, -a, -um — wished for, desired
pro re nata — according to the circumstances
distribuo, -uere, -ui, -utum — to distribute
promontorium, -ii — promontory
auster, -stri — south
titulus, -i — title, honor
consecro, 1 — to consecrate, dedicate
aquilonaris, -e — northern
Sancto Michaeli — to St. Michael, the archangel. One of the tracts
of land forming administrative units of the early settlement was
called 'St. Michael's Hundred'.
indigito, 1 — to name
Maius iucundiusve ...aspexi — refers to the Potomac River
rivulus, -i — small brook, rivulet
inficio, -ficere — to taint
palus, -udis, f. — swamp, marsh, bog
solidus, -a, -um — solid, firm
utrinque — on both sides
assurgo, 3 — to rise up
decens, -ntis — proper, fine
clausus, -a, -um — closed, made inaccesssible
vepretum, -i — thornhedge, bramble-thicket
subnascor, 3 (dep.) — to grow up (out of), grow underneath
surculus, -i — young shoot, sprout
quasi — as if
laxus, -a, -um — wide, loose, spacious
consero, -serere, -sevi, -situm — to sow, plant
quadriga, -ae — chariot drawn by four horses
agito, 1 — to drive

INDIGENARUM METUS ET ADMIRATIO.
INSULAE ARDEARUM.
LINTEA DEPERDITA

ostium, -ii — mouth (of a river)
indigena, -ae — native
conspicio, -spicere, -spexi, -spectum — to catch sight of, behold,
perceive
ardeo, -ere, arsi — to burn, glow
illis = ab illis
conspecta fuit = conspecta est
nuntius, -ii — messenger
hinc inde — on this side and on that, from this side and from that
canoa, canoae — canoe
advento, 1 — to come near, approach

labitur, profundus quattuor, quinque,
695 sex et septem orgyis, piscibus cum favet
annus scatens. Iucundiorem aeque
lapsum vix invenies. Cedit tamen
fluvio Patomeach, cui nomen a Sancto
Gregorio indidimus.

700   Iam enim optata potiti regione,
nomina pro re nata distribuebamus.
Et quidem promontorium quod est ad
austrum titulo Sancti Gregorii
consecravimus, aquilonare Sancto
705 Michaeli, in honorem omnium
angelorum Marilandiae indigitantes.
Maius iucundiusve flumen aspexi
numquam; Thamesis illi comparatus
vix rivulus videri potest; nullis inficitur
710 paludibus, sed solida utrinque terra
assurgunt decentes arborum silvae, non
clausae vepretis vel subnascentibus
surculis, sed quasi manu laxa consitae
ut libere quadrigam inter medias
715 arbores agitare possis.

26 • INDIGENARUM METUS ET ADMIRATIO. INSULAE ARDEARUM. LINTEA DEPERDITA

    In ipso ostio fluminis armatos
indigenas conspeximus. Ea nocte ignes
tota regione arserunt; et, quoniam
720 nunquam illis tam magna navis
conspecta fuit, nuntii hinc inde missi
narrabant, canoam insulae similem
adventasse; tot homines quot in silvis

694 quatuor *ms* 695 orygis *ms* 697 Patomeach fluvius
sive Sancti Gregorii *in marg. sin.* 700 inquit horum
scriptor ac testis *altera manus annotavit* 706 Promontorium
eiusdem Michaelis *in marg. dext.* 708 nunquam *ms*
713 sarcubis *ms* 721 Indigenarum metus et admiratio
in marg. dext.

procedo, -cedere, -cessi, -cessum — to advance, continue
insulae Ardearum — the Heron Islands (small islands in the Potomac River)
inauditus, -a, -um — unheard of
examen, -inis, n. — swarm, throng, crowd
volucris, -is — bird
appello, 1 — to address, call, name
descendo, -scendere, -scendi, -scensum — to descend, to leave the ship
insula Sancti Clementis — St. Clement's Island, also known as Blackstone Island, is the southern-most of this group of small islands. It was probably so named, because an event facilitating the departure of the *Ark* and the *Dove* had taken place on St.Clement's Day the previous year (see chapter 1).
insula Sanctae Ceciliae — St. Cecilia's Island, now called St. Margaret's Island. The voyage had begun on Cecilia's Day, 1633 (see chapter 1).
insula Sanctae Catharinae — St. Catherine's Island
vadum, -i — shallow, ford
declivis, -e — inclined downwards, sloping
ancilla, -ae — maid-servant
lavo, 1 — to wash
exscendo, -scendere, -scendi, -scensum — here: to leave the ship
linter, -tris, f. — boat, skiff
submergo, -mergere, -mersi, mersum — to plunge under, sink
lintea, -orum (n. pl.) — linen (clothes)
deperdo, -perdere, -perdidi, perditum — to lose
iactura, -ae — loss
mediocris, -e — moderate, ordinary, 'small'
abundo, 1, with abl. — to abound in
cedrus, -i, f. — cedar
saxifragium -ii — sassafras (had been praised for its great medicinal value by Monardes, a leading physician at Seville in the second half of the sixteenth century)
herba, -ae — green plant, herb
flos, floris, m. — flower
acetarium, -ii — salad
nux, nucis, f. — nut-tree
silvestris, -e — of the woods, wild
iuglans, -glandis, f. — nut
praedurus, -a, -um — very hard
spissus, -a, -um — thick
putamen, -inis, n. — shell
nucleus, -i — kernel (of a nut)
mirus, -a, -um — wonderful
iugerum, -i (gen. plu. iugerum) — measure of land; here: acre
latitudo, -inis, f. — breadth, extent, size
plantatio, -onis, f. — plantation, settlement
castrum, -i — fort, fortress
aedifico, 1 — to build
exterus, -a, -um — foreign, strange
commercium, -ii — trade, traffic
tutor, 1 (dep.) — to protect, watch, keep
angustus, -a, -um — short, narrow
traiectus, -us, m. — passage, crossing-over

PRIMA MISSA. CRUX ERECTA

dies Annunciationis Sanctissimae Virginis Mariae — the Feast of the Annunciation (March 25th). It celebrates the announcement, made by the angel Gabriel to the Virgin Mary, that the Son of God will become man and is to be born of Mary. March 25th is still celebrated as Maryland Day.
lito, 1 — to offer Mass
antea — before
id...factum — supply: est
sacrificium, -ii — here: mass, service

arbores. Processimus tamen ad insulas
725 Ardearum, sic dictas ab inauditis
examinibus huiusmodi volucrum.
Primam quae occurrit Sancti Clementis
nomine appellavimus; secundam
Sanctae Catharinae; tertiam Sanctae
730 Ceciliae. Descendimus primum ad
Sancti Clementis, ad quam nisi vado
non patet accessus propter declive littus.
Hic ancillae, quae ad lavandum
exscenderunt, inverso lintre paene
735 submersae sunt, magna parte meorum
etiam linteorum deperdita, iactura in
his partibus non mediocri.

Abundat haec insula cedro,
saxifragio, herbis et floribus ad omnis
740 generis acetaria componenda, nuce
etiam silvestri, quae iuglandem fert
praeduram, spisso putamine, nucleo
parvo sed mire grato. Cum tamen
quadringentorum tantum iugerum
745 [esset] latitudine, visa est non ampla
satis futura sedes novae plantationi,
quaesitus est tamen locus castro
aedificando ad prohibendos exteros
fluvii commercio finesque tutandos; is
750 enim erat angustissimus fluminis
traiectus.

27 • PRIMA MISSA. CRUX ERECTA

755 Die Annunciationis Sanctissimae
Virginis Mariae primum in hac insula
litavimus: id in hac caeli regione
numquam antea factum. Sacrificio

---

726 Insulae Ardearum *in marg. dext.* 729 Catherinae *ms.*
733 Lintea deperdita *in marg. dext.* 741 sylvestri *ms*
756 23 anno 1634 758 id *altera manus inseruit* 757 coeli *ms*
nunquam *ms*

perago, -agere, -egi, actum — to complete, accomplish
humerus, -i — shoulder
ingens, -ntis — enormous, huge
dedolo, 1 — to hew out
designo, 1 — to mark out, indicate, designate
procedo, 3 — prodeed, advance
commissarius, -ii — offical, governor's associate
* catholicus, -i — (Roman) Catholic
trophaeum, -i — trophy, monument
Servator, -oris — Savior
erigo, -ere, -rexi, -rectum — to erect
litaniae Sanctae Crucis — the Litany of the Holy Cross (a liturgical prayer)
flecto, -ere, flexi, flectum — to bend
genu, -us, n. — knee
commotio, -onis, f. — emotion
recito, 1 — to recite

CONVENITUR REX PATOMEACH ET IMPERATOR

Pascatavvaye — 'of Piscataway', a village of the Piscataways further up the Potomac. The chieftain of the Piscataways, here referred to as 'emperor', was indeed the paramount chief of a loose federation of chiefdoms in Maryland.
complures, -ium — several
pareo, 2 — to obey, be subject to
regulus, -i — petty king, prince, ruler
explico, 1 — to explain
concilio, 1 — to reconcile, win over
voluntas, -atis, f. — will, wish
ingressus, -us — entry, access
conduco, -ere, -duxi, -ductum — to hire, procure
navi — ablative of navis
anchora, -ae — anchor
Patomeach — Patawomeck, an Indian village situated on the southern, i.e., the Virginian shore of the Potomac. Since the chief of the Patawomeck Indians ruled only over his own chiefdom, he is called 'king' by White, while the paramount chief of several Maryland chiefdoms is called 'emperor' (see above).
circumago, -ere, -egi, -actum — to turn around
australis, -e — southern
exscendo, -scendere, -scendi, -scensum — to ascend, go up from the coast
ad australem partem fluminis exscendit — 'he went up from the coast on the southern shore of the river'
barbarus, -i — foreigner, savage
interior, -ius, -ioris — inner, interior, inland
comperio, -perire, -peri, -pertum — to learn
civitas, -atis, f. — here: town, village
desumo, -sumere, -sumpsi, -sumptum — to take out, select
tutor, -oris, m. — guardian
patruus, -i, m. — uncle
vicis (genit.) — one's place, office (vices = acc. plu.)
puerique vices in regno habebat — 'ruled in his (the boy's) place'
Pater Altham — Father John Altham, one of the three Jesuits accompanying the expedition to Maryland
etenim — for indeed
etiamnum — still
sarcina, -ae — load, cargo
gentilis, -e — of a gens or country; here: pagan, heathen
identidem — repeatedly
agnosco, 3 — to recognize, admit, acknowledge
edoceo, -docere, -docui, -doctum — to inform fully

760 peracto, sublata in humero ingenti cruce quam ex arbore dedolaveramus, ad locum designatum ordine procedentes, praefecto et commissariis ceterisque catholicis adiutantibus, trophaeum Christo Servatori ereximus,
765 litaniis Sanctae Crucis humiliter flexis genibus magna animorum commotione recitatis.

28 · CONVENITUR REX PATOMEACH ET IMPERATOR

Cum autem intellexisset praefectus
770 imperatori Pascatavvaye complures parere regulos, illum adire statuit ut, explicata itineris nostri causa et eius unius conciliata voluntate, facilior ad ceterorum animos pateret ingressus.
775 Itaque, iuncta celoci nostrae altera quam in Virginia conduxerat, et navi in anchoris relicta ad Sanctum Clementem, cursu circumacto, ad australem partem fluminis exscendit.
780 Cumque barbaros ad interiora fugisse comperisset, progressus est ad civitatem, quae a flumine desumpto nomine Patomeach etiam dicitur. Hic regi puero tutor erat patruus nomine
785 Archihu puerique vices in regno habebat, vir gravis et prudens. Is Patri Nostro Altham, qui comes additus erat praefecto (me etenim etiamnum detinebat ad sarcinas), quaedam [quae]
790 per interpretem de gentilium erroribus explicanti libenter aures dabat, suos identidem agnoscens; utque edoctus

759 Prima missa *in marg. sin.* 762 Crux erecta *in marg. sin.*
763 caeterisque *ms* 774 caeterorum *ms*
786 Convenitur rex Patomeach *in marg. sin.*

benevolentia, -ae — good-will
gratia (postpos.) with gen. — on account of, for the sake of
appello, -pellere, -puli, -pulsum — to put in, land
civilis, -e — civilized
praeceptum, -i — rules, precepts, instruction
longinquus, -a, -um — distant, remote
commodum, -i — advantage
imbuo, 3 — to instruct
impartio, -ire, -ivi, -itum — to share something with a person, impart
monstro, 1 — to show
protestans, -ntis — Protestant
pro tempore — 'because of the shortness of time', 'at the time'
dissero, 3 — to discuss
id mihi ex animo accidit — 'this is just what I want'
mensa, -ae — table
assecla, -ae, m. — attendant, follower
venatum ire — to go hunting
ad Pascatavvaye — 'to Piscataway' (see above). The Piscataways belonged to the Algonquian linguistic family and were under attack from the Susquehannocks, an Iroquois tribe. The chief probably expected, and rightly so, that the English settlers would become allies in this struggle. Father White later moved to a Piscataway village, and shortly afterwards the chief, or Tayac, Kittamaquund, converted with his family and part of his tribe.
arcubus, from: **arcus, -us, m.** — bow
instructus, -a, -um — armed (with)
celocem conscendere — to come on board the pinnace
benevolus, -a, -um — kind, obliging, well-meaning
facultas, -atis, f. — opportunity, power, permission
facultatem...habitandi — 'permission to settle in whatever part of his empire we wished'
vigilibus...admiscebant — 'were becoming more familiar with our guards'
excubias agere — to keep guard
lignator, -oris, m. — wood-cutter
aphractus, -i — long, undecked boat
tabulis costisque solutis — 'with the boards and ribs dissassembled'
aedifico, 1 — to build
repens, -ntis — sudden, unexpected
insultus, -us — attack
tutor, 1 (dep.) — to protect
singulus, -a, -um — single
ubinam — where
excresco, -crescere, -crevi, -cretum — to grow up
dedolo, 1 — to hew out
excido, -cidere, -cidi, -cisum — to cut out
quemadmodum — as, just as

nos non belli causa, sed benevolentiae
gratia eo appulisse, ut gentem rudem
795 civilibus praeceptis imbueremus et
viam ad caelum aperiremus, simul
regionum longinquarum commoda iis
impartituros, gratos advenisse
monstravit. Interpres erat ex
800 protestantibus Virginiae. Itaque, cum
plura pro tempore disserere non posset
Pater, promisit se non ita multo post
reversurum. Id mihi ex animo accidit,
inquit Archihu; una mensa utemur, mei
805 quoque asseclae pro te venatum ibunt,
eruntque inter nos omnia communia.

Hinc itum ad Pascatavvaye, ubi
omnes ad arma convolarant. Quingenti
circiter arcubus instructi in littore cum
810 imperatore constiterant. Signis pacis
datis, imperator metu posito celocem
conscendit, et, audito nostrorum
benevolo erga eas gentes animo,
facultatem dedit qua imperii eius parte
815 vellemus habitandi.

Interdum dum praefectus apud
imperatorem in itinere esset, barbari ad
Sanctum Clementem audentiores facti
se vigilibus nostris familiarius
820 admiscebant. Excubias enim interdiu
noctuque agebamus, tum ut lignatores
nostros, tum ut aphractum, quem
tabulis costisque solutis allatum
aedificabamus, ab repentibus insultibus
825 tutaremur. Voluptati erat audire
admirantes singula: in primis ubinam
terrarum tanta arbor excrevissset, ex
qua tam immensa moles navis
dedolaretur; excisam enim
830 arbitrabantur quemadmodum Indicae

---

796 coelum *ms* 809 Et imperator *in marg. sin.*

Indica canoa — Indian canoe
truncus, -i — trunk
tormentum, -i — cannon
attonitus, -a, -um — stunned, terrified
quippe — certainly
vocalis, -e — resounding
tonitruum, -i — thunder

CIVITAS SANCTAE MARIAE.
FLUVIUS SANCTI GEORGII.
AUGUSTA CAROLINA

adhibeo, -hibere, -hibui, -hibitum — to employ
Henricus Fleet capitaneus — Captain Henry Fleet, a fur trader, whom Leonard Calvert met during his search for an Indian chief. Fleet had been captured by the Anacostian Indians and remained among them for several years, learning their language and customs. After escaping captivity, he left for England, but returned again to live among the Yaocomico Indians and traded extensively with them in furs.
commoror, 1 (dep.) — to stay
* barbarus, -i — foreign, savage
perfamiliaris, -is — a very close friend
Clabornus — as secretary of Virginia William Claiborne had fought vigorously against Lord Baltimore's charter. The grant affected him personally, as he had established a fort and fur trading post on Kent Island, a large island in the Chesapeake Bay. Though the island was clearly within Lord Baltimore's territory, Claiborne refused to acknowledge Governor Calverts's jurisdiction and continued to cause problems for the Maryland colony for many years.
seduco, -ducere, -duxti, -ductum — to mislead, deceive
sinister, -tra, -trum — unfavorable, wrong, adverse
infensus, -a, -um — hostile
efficio, -ficere, -feci, -fectum — to make
accendo, -cendere, -cendi, -censum — to inflame, excite
monstro, 1 — to show
benignitas, -atis, f. — here: charm, pleasantness
a Sancto Clemente...illapsi sumus — 'we advanced from St. Clement's Island about nine leagues [down the Potomac] and then sailed into the mouth of a river on the northern shoreline [of the Potomac]'
leuca, -ae — league (nautical measure of distance, about three and a half miles)
a Sancto Georgio — it is now called St. Mary's River
indo, -dere, -didi, -ditum — to give, confer
auster, -tri, m. — south
milliarium, -ii — mile
procurro, 3 — to run forward
salsedo, -inis, f. — saltiness
marinus, -a, -um — of the sea
exuo, 3, with abl.— to strip, deprive of
Thamesis, -is — the river Thames (on which London is located)
viso, 3 — to look at, see
sinus, -us, m. — bay
immensus, -a, -um — immense, vast
capax, -acis, with gen. — able to hold
Yaocomico — 'of Yaocomico,' a village on what is now called the St. Mary's River in southern Maryland. Since Captain Henry Fleet had lived among the Yaocomico Indians for years, he was, of course, familiar with this area and may have known about their intention to leave as well.
exscendo, -scendere, -scendi, -scensum — to ascend, to go up from the sea-coast inland

canoae ex uno aliquo arboris trunco. Tormenta maiora attonitos omnes tenebant, haud paulo quippe vocaliora erant stridulis ipsorum arcubus, et
835 tonitruo paria.

29 • CIVITAS SANCTAE MARIAE. FLUVIUS SANCTI GEORGII. AUGUSTA CAROLINA

Praefectus socium itineris ad imperatorem adhibuerat Henricum Fleet capitaneum ex iis qui in Virginia
840 commorantur, hominem barbaris in primis gratum et linguae locorumque peritum. Hic initio nobis perfamiliaris, deinde Claborni cuiusdam sinistris seductus consiliis infensissimus effectus,
845 indigenarum animos qua arte potest adversus nos accendit. Interim tamen, dum inter nos amicus ageret, sedem praefecto monstravit qualem vix Europa meliorem loci benignitate
850 ostendere potest. Igitur, a Sancto Clemente novem circiter leucas progressi ad aquilonem, fluminis ostio illapsi sumus, cui a Sancto Georgio nomen indidimus. Id flumen ab austro
855 ad aquilonem ad viginti circiter milliaria procurrit antequam salsedine marina exuatur, Thamesi non dissimile. In eius ostio duo visuntur sinus 300 navium immensae molis capaces.
860 Sinum unum Sancto Georgio consecravimus, alterum interius Beatissimae Virgini Mariae. Laeva pars fluminis sedes erat regis Yaocomico; nos ad dexteram exscendimus, et ad mille

---

837 Civitas Sanctae Mariae *in marg. sin.* **854** Fluvius Sancti Georgii *in marg. sin.* **862** Leva *ms*

avello, -vellere, -vulsi, -vulsum — remove
civitas, -atis, f. — here: city
designo, 1 — to plan, indicate, elect, designate
nomen a Sancta Maria posuimus — St. Mary's City was the first capital of Maryland. Scholars are not absolutely certain where the expedition landed and where the first fort was located. However, there is clear archaeological evidence of several seventeenth-century buildings on a promontory called Church Point today, in the area of Historic St. Mary's City, near St. Mary's College of Maryland. St. Mary's City never developed into the urban center envisioned by its founders, but the area still offers visitors fascinating archaeological sites and artifacts as well as site reconstructions.
species, -ei — here: appearance, notion, idea
iniuria, -ae — injury, injustice, wrong
inimicitia, -ae — enmity
praeverto, 3 — to anticipate, forestall, prevent
appendo, -pendere, -pendi, -pensum — to weigh to, deal out
commutatio, -onis — exchange
securis, -is, f. — axe, hatchet
ascia, -ae — carpenter's axe
rastrum, -i - hoe, rake
mensura, -ae — measure, yard
pannus, -i — (piece of) cloth
emo, emere, -emi, emptum — to buy, purchase
milliare, -is, n. — mile

SASQUEHANOES

Sasquehanoes — the Susquehannocks belonged to the Iroquois language family and originally lived along the Susquehanna River, but were feared by the Algonquian tribes of Maryland because of their raids into this area. From 1642 on the Maryland colonists, too, found themselves at war with the Susquehannocks, who also had trade relations with European settlers.
assuetus, -a, -um — accustomed to
Yaocomico — 'of Yaocomico'
prae ceteris — above all
infestus, -a, -um — hostile, dangerous
frequens, -ntis — frequent
incursus, -us, m. — attack, assault
depopulor, 1 (dep.) — to lay waste, ravage, destroy
adigo, 3 — to drive, force, compel
prompte — promptly, quickly
impetro, 1 — to obtain (by asking)
adminiculum, -i — support, aid, help
aperio, -ire — to open
migrant...quotidie — 'daily some of them depart'
novale, -is, n. — cultivated field, crop
nobisque...novalia — this arrangement, along with the abundance of fish, fowl, and deer prevented famine and even food shortages, which were not uncommon in other North American colonies.
miraculum, -i — wonderful thing, miracle
adversum, with acc. — against
agnus, -i — lamb
permitto, -mittere, -misi, -missum — to give up, yield
digitus, -i — finger
meditor, 1 (dep.) — to think about (doing), intend
adhuc — still, even now
habitatio, -onis, f. — dwelling, habitation

865 passus a littore avulsi civitati designatae nomen a Sancta Maria posuimus; utque omnem speciem iniuriae inimicitiarumque occasionem praeverteremus, appensis in commutationem securibus,
870 asciis, rastris et mensuris aliquot panni, emimus a rege triginta terrae illius milliaria, cui regioni Augusta Carolina iam nomen est.

30 · SASQUEHANOES

875 Sasquehanoes, gens bellis assueta, regi Yaocomico prae ceteris infesta, frequentibus incursibus omnem depopulatur agrum, et incolas ad alias quaerendas sedes periculi metu adigit.
880 Haec causa est cur tam prompte partem eius regni impetravimus, Deo viam legi suae et lumini aeterno his adminiculis aperiente. Migrant alii atque alii quotidie, nobisque relinquunt domos,
885 agros, novalia. Id profecto miraculo simile est, homines barbaros, paucis antea diebus in armis adversum nos paratos, tam facile se nobis velut agnos permittere, nobis se suaque tradere.
890 Digitus Dei est hic, et magnum aliquod emolumentum huic nationi meditatur Deus. Paucis tamen quibusdam permittitur adhuc sua inter nos habitatio in annum proximum. Tum vero liber
895 nobis relinquendus est ager.

---

872 Augusta Carolina *in marg. dext.* 875 Sasquehanoes *in marg. dext.* 876 Yaocomio *ms* caeteris *ms*

INDIGENARUM SPECIES. VESTES. DOMUS

* **indigena, -ae** — native. White here describes the Yaocomico Indians.
statura, -ae — stature, height
procerus, -a, -um — tall
decens, -ntis — proper, fine
cutis, -is, f. — skin
subfuscus, -a, -um, — brownish, dark
rubeus, -a, -um — red
mistus = mixtus, -a, -um — mixed, prepared
oleum, -i — oil
inficio, -ficere — to tinge, stain, paint
culex, -icis, m. — gnat, mosquito
teter = taeter, -tra, trum — hideous, ugly
commodum, -i — comfort
intentus, -a, -um — anxious for, intent on
deturpo, 1 — to make ugly, disfigure
nasus, -i — nose
sursum — upwards
caeruleum, -i — blue color
deorsum — downwards
rubicundus, -a, -um — red (color)
sane — indeed, really, to be sure
foedus, -a, -um — horrible, disgusting
terrificus, -a, -um — frightful, terrible
barba, -ae — beard
ultimus, -a, -um — extreme
pigmentum, -i — pigment, color
simulo, 1 — to represent
linea, -ae — line
extimus, -a, -um — outermost
labium, ii — lip
auris, -is, f. — ear
produco, -ducere, -duxi, -ductum — to bring out, draw
caesaries, -ei, f. — hair
plerumque — for the most part, generally
niger, -gra, -grum — black
nutrio, -ire — here: to grow
nodus, -i — knot
circumduco, -ducere, -duxi, -ductum — to take around
vitta, -ae — ribbon, band
astringo, 3 — to tighten, draw together
monile, -is, n. — ornament
frons, -ntis, f. — forehead
praefero, -ferre — to show, display
figura, -ae — form, shape
cupreus, -a, -um — of copper
collum, -i — neck
munio, -ire — to surround
vitreus, -a, -um — of glass
globulus, -i — bead
filum, -i — thread
insero, -serere, -serui, -sertum — to connect
torquis, -is, m. and f. — necklace
vilis, -e — cheap, worth little
ut plurimum — for the most part
pellis, is, f. — hide, skin
cervinus, -a, -um — of a deer
velum, -i — here: covering
tergum, -i — back
pallium, -ii — mantle
cingo, -ere, -cinxi, -cinctum — to surround, equip
umbilicus, -i — navel, middle (of the body)
perizoma, -atis, n. (perizomatis: abl. plu.) — apron
nudus, -a, um — naked
impubes, -is — youthful, unmarried
vagor, 1 (dep.) — to wander, rove
planta, -ae — here: sole of the foot
spina, -ae — thorn, prickle
tribulus, -i — thorny plant
calco, 1 — to tread, trample on
illaesus, -a, -um — without being hurt
cubitum, -i — a cubit (measure of length, ca. 18 inches)
albus, -a, -um — white
praeacutus, -a, -um — very sharp
silex, -icis, m. — hard stone, flint

31 • INDIGENARUM SPECIES. VESTES. DOMUS

Indigenae statura sunt procera et decenti, cute a natura subfusca, quam
900 colore plerumque rubeo misto oleo inficientes, ut culices arceant, tetriorem reddunt, commodo suo magis intenti quam decori. Vultum aliis etiam coloribus deturpant a naso sursum
905 caerulei, deorsum rubicundi vel contra, variis et sane foedis terrificisque modis. Et, quoniam barba in ultimam prope aetatem carent, pigmentis barbam simulant, lineis varii coloris ab extimis
910 labiis ad aures productis. Caesariem, quam plerumque nigram nutriunt, in nodum ad sinistram aurem circum-ductam vitta astringunt, addito aliquo, quod apud ipsos in pretio sit, monili.
915 Quidam in fronte praeferunt piscis figuram cupream. Colla muniunt vitreis globulis filo insertis more torquium, quamquam hi globuli viliores apud ipsos esse incipiunt et
920 commercio minus utiles.

Vestiuntur ut plurimum pelle cervina vel similis generis velo, quod a tergo fluit in modum pallii, cincti ad [ad] umbilicum perizomatis, cetera
925 nudi. Impubes pueri puellaeque nulla re tecti vagantur. Plantis pedum velut cornu duris spinas tribulosque calcant illaesi. Arma sunt arcus et sagittae duos cubitos longae, cornu cervino vel albo
930 praeacutoque silice armatae; has tanta

---

898 Indigenarum species *in marg. dext.* **923** Vestes *in marg. sin.* **924** caeteri *ms*

libro, 1 — to hurl, shoot
passer, -eris, m. — sparrow, small bird
eminus — at a distance, from a distance
configo, 3 — to pierce through
peritia, -ae — experience, skill
exerceo, 2 — to exercise, train
lorum, -i — strap, whip, thong of leather
sublimis, -e — high
impello, -pellere, -puli, -pulsum — to drive against, set in motion, release
nervus, -i — string, bowstring
infigo — 3 — to fasten, thrust in
contentus, -a, -um — stretched, strained, tightly strung
meta, -ae — goal, target
ferio, -ire — to strike, hit
sciurus, -i — squirrel
perdix, -icis — partridge
pullus Indicus — turkey
venor, 1 (dep.) — to hunt
ingens, -ntis — vast, enormous
expedio, -ire — to get ready, procure
alimentum, -i — food
venatus, -us, m. — hunting
quamquam...audeamus — translate as if **audeamus** were indicative
habito, 1 — to inhabit
ovalis, -e — oval
oblongus, -a, -um — oblong. White aptly describes the so-called 'long-house'.
constructus, -a, -um — constructed
fenestra, -ae — window
cubitalis, -e — one cubit long
fumus, -i — smoke
inservio, -ire — to serve
pavimentum, -i — pavement, floor
accendo, 3 — to kindle
princeps, -cipis — first, foremost
velut — 'something like', 'as it were'
conclave, -is, n. — room, chamber
lectus, -i — bed
fulcrum, -i — post, foot
asser, -eris, m. — stake, pole
superpono, -ponere, -posui, -positum — to place over
insterno, -sternere, -stravi, -stratum — to spread over, cover
casula, -ae — little hut, cottage
obtingo, -tingere, -tigi — to happen, fall (to somebody)
sat — sufficiently, enough
commode — comfortably
laxus, -a, um — wide, spacious
sacellum, -i — chapel
decens, -ntis — proper, fine
instruo, -struere, -struxi, -structum — to furnish
navigatio, -onis, f. — voyage
annuo, 3 — to nod assent, agree, assent
coeptum, -i — a beginning, undertaking

arte librant ut passerem eminus medium configant, utque se ad peritiam exerceant, lorum in sublime iaciunt, tum impulsam nervo sagittam infigunt
935 antequam decidat. Arcu quoniam non admodum contento utuntur, metam longe positam ferire non possunt. His armis vivunt et quotidie per agros et silvas sciuros, perdices, pullos Indicos
940 ferasque venantur. Horum enim omnium ingens est copia, quamquam nondum nobis ipsi expedire alimenta venatu audeamus metu insidiarum.

Domos habitant ovali forma
945 oblonga constructas, novem vel decem pedes altas. In has lumen a tecto admittitur fenestra cubitali; illa fumo etiam auferendo inservit; nam ignem medio in pavimento accendunt, et circa
950 ignem dormiunt. Reges tamen et principes viri sua habent velut conclavia et lectum quatuor fulcris in terram adactis et asseribus superpositis instratum. Mihi et sociis ex his casulis
955 una obtigit, in qua sat pro tempore commode habemur, donec aedificia parentur laxiora. Illam primum Marilandiae sacellum dixeris, quamquam haud paulo decentius
960 instructum quam cum ab Indis habitabatur. Proxima navigatione, si Deus coeptis annuat, non deerunt nostris quae ceteris in domibus sunt usui necessaria.

---

939 sylvas *ms* 946 Domus *in marg. dext.* 951 habeant *ms* 954 Mihi et sociis *altera manus delevit et explevit verbo* Nostris 959 quanquam *ms* 963 caeteris *ms*

INDOLES. VICTUS

indoles, -is, f. — disposition, character
ingenuus, -a, -um — noble, frank
gustus, -us, m. — sense of taste
odoratus, -us, m. — sense of smell
visus, -us, m. — seeing, sight
victito, 1 — to live (on)
puls, pultis, f. — paste, mush
triticum, -i — here: corn
venatus, us, m. — hunting
aucupium, -ii — bird-catching, fowling
assequor, 3 (dep.) — to reach by following, attain
potio, -onis, f. — drink
degusto, 1 — to taste
Angli, -orum — the English
inficio, -ficere, -feci, fectum — to corrupt, taint
castitas, -atis, f. — chastity
attineo, 2 (**ad** with acc.) — to pertain to
adverto, -vertere, -verti, -versum — to perceive
femina, -ae — woman
sapio, sapere (with acc.) — (to taste, smell of =) savor of
quotidie = cottidie — daily, every day
consortium, -ii — partnership, company
gaudeo, 2 — to delight (in), find pleasure (in)
sponte — willingly, of one's own accord
vultus, -us, m. — expression (of the face)
hilaritas, -atis, f. — cheerfulness
vultu ad hilaritatem composito — 'with a cheerful expression'
venor, 1 (dep.) — to hunt
piscor, 1 (dep.) — to fish
libum, -i — cake, bread
ostreum, -i — oyster
coctus, -a, -um — cooked, boiled
assus, -a, -um — roasted
idque — supply: faciunt
vernaculus, -a, um — native
hactenus — so far, up to this point
utcumque — in whatever manner
aspectus, us, m. — appearance
in universum — 'towards all'
rependo, 3 — to repay, return
temere — rashly, thoughtlessly
motus, -us, m. —impulse, passion, emotion
momentum, -i — importance
aliquando —sometime, at one time
silent cogitabundi — 'they think it over in silence'
aliquandiu = aliquamdiu — for some time
aiunt — 'they say yes', 'they agree'
propositum, -i — intention, resolution, purpose
profecto — really, actually

965

32 • INDOLES. VICTUS

Gentis indoles ingenua est et laeta et
quae rem   probe capiat cum proponitur; gustu excellunt et odoratu, visu
etiam Europaeos superant. Victitant
970 plerumque pulte, quem pone et omini
appellant; utraque ex tritico conficitur,
adduntque interdum piscem vel quod
venatu aucupioque assecuti sunt.
Cavent sibi quam maxime a vino et
975 potionibus calidis, neque adducuntur
facile ut eas degustent, nisi quos Angli
suis vitiis infecerint. Quod ad
castitatem attinet fateor me nondum
advertisse in viro vel femina actionem
980 ullam, quae vel levitatem saperet;
quotidie tamen nobiscum et apud nos
sunt, et nostro gaudent uti consortio.
Accurrunt sponte, vultu ad hilaritatem
composito, et offerunt quae venati vel
985 piscati fuerint, liba etiam aliquando et
ostrea cocta vel assa, idque paucis
invitati linguae ipsis vernaculae verbis,
quae per signa hactenus utcumque
didicimus. Plures ducunt uxores,
990 integram tamen servant fidem
coniugalem. Mulierum aspectus gravis
est et modestus. In universum liberales
nutriunt animos; quicquid beneficii
contuleris, rependunt. Nil temere
995 decernunt aut subito arrepti motu
animi, sed ratione; ideo cum quidquam
momenti aliquando proponitur, silent
aliquandiu cogitabundi, tum aiunt
breviter aut negant, et propositi sunt
1000 tenacissimi. Hi profecto si semel

966 Indoles *in marg. dext.* **968** Victus *in marg. dext.*
979 faemina *ms*

imbuo, 3 — to imbue, instruct
christianus, -a, -um — Christian
linguae his regionibus usitatae defectum — 'our ignorance of the language spoken in these parts'
humanitas, -atis, f. — 'humanity'; **humanitas** is a term which encompasses a wide range of meanings: kindness, compassion, culture, refinement, etc.
cultor, -oris — cultivator, observer
evado, 3 — to become, prove to be
mirus, -a, -um — amazing, astonishing
desiderium, -ii — desire
civilis, -e — polite, civilized
conversatio, -onis, f. — social intercourse, conversation
indumentum, -i — garment
pridem — long ago
vestis, -is, f. — garment, clothing
fuissent usi = **usi essent**
avaritia, -ae — greed, avarice
mercator, -oris, m. — merchant
pannus, -i — cloth
castor, -oris, m. beaver
commuto, 1, with abl. — to exchange (something for)
unusquisque — every single
imitor, 1 (dep.) — to imitate

RELIGIO

idioma, -atis, n. — language
ignoratio, onis, f. — ignorance
facit — 'is the reason'
porro — further
idiomatis...constet — White's remarks on native religion are a very important source on this subject. Though Jesuits' reports were, of course, colored by the missionaries' own beliefs, they reflect the Jesuits' extraordinary efforts to understand foreign cultures, and convey more information on native religions than other documents.
protestans, -ntis — Protestant
fido, 3 — to trust
raptim — hastily, hurriedly
agnosco, 3 — to acknowledge
externus, -a, -um outside, external
exhibeo, 2, — to show, display, offer
placo, 1 — to reconcile, appease
phanaticus, -a, -um — inspired, frezied, evil
Ochre — Virginian sources, too, mention such a spirit, called 'Oke,' or 'Okee.'
ut ne = **ne**
mirus, -a, -um — wonderful
Barcluxem — should probably read: **Patuxent** — 'of the Patuxent.' The Patuxent were one of the Lower Western Shore Algonquian tribes of Maryland. Their chief Macquacomen became very well disposed towards the Jesuits and gave them a tract of cultivated land during the early years of their mission.
constitutus, -a, -um — settled, arranged, agreed upon
pagus, -i — district
femina, -ae — woman
ingens, -ntis — enormous
iunior, -oris — young
pone — behind, at the back
provectus, -a, -um — advanced in age
adeps, adipis — fat (the soft fat of animals)
cervinus, -a, -um — of a deer
intervallum, -i — interval

christianis praeceptis imbuantur (et quidem nihil obstare videtur, praeter linguae his regionibus usitatae defectum) virtutis humanitatisque

1005 cultores egregii evadent. Miro tenentur desiderio civilis conversationis Europaeorumque indumentorum; iamque pridem vestibus fuissent usi, ni avaritia mercatorum obstitisset, qui

1010 pannos nisi castore non commutant. Castorem vero unusquisque venari non potest. Absit ut horum avaritiam nos imitemur.

33 · RELIGIO

1015   Idiomatis ignoratio facit ut quid porro de religione sentiant nondum constet; interpretibus enim protestantibus minus fidimus. Haec pauca raptim didicimus. Unum Deum coeli

1020 agnoscunt, quem Deum nostrum vocant; nullum tamen honorem externum illi exhibent; omni vero ratione placare conantur phanaticum quendam spiritum quem Ochre

1025 nominant, ut ne noceat. Frumentum, ut audio, et ignem colunt, ut deos humano generi mire beneficos. Hanc ceremoniam quidam e nostris in templo Barcluxem vidisse se narrant. Die

1030 constituto e pluribus pagis convenere circa ingentem ignem omnes omnium aetatum viri feminaeque; proxime ad ignem stabant iuniores, pone illos provectiores. Tum adipe cervina in

1035 ignem coniecta et sublatis in coelum manibus et vocibus clamabant omnes: taho taho. Intervallo facto profert unus

1015 Religio *in marg. dext.* 1032 faeminaeque *ms*

pera, -ae — bag
tubus, -i — pipe
pulvis, —veris, m. — powder
nostras, -atis, m. countryman
exsugo, 3 — to suck out, smoke
fumus, -i — smoke
tobaccus, -i — tobacco
alterno, 1 — to alternate, chant alternately
circulus, -i — circle
eximo, 3 — to take out
asto, 1 — to stand by
distribuo, 3 — to distribute
accendo, -cendere, -cendi, -censum — to light
singulus, -a, -um — one at a time, each
consecro, 1 — to consecrate
notitia, -ae — notion, conception
diluvium, -ii — flood, deluge

aliquis bene magnam peram; in pera est tubus et pulvis, quem potre nominant;
1040 tubus est quali nostrates utuntur ad exsugendum fumum tabacci, sed multo maior. Igitur pera circa ignem fertur, sequentibus pueris et puellis et voce satis grata alternantibus: taho taho.
1045 Circulo peracto, eximitur tubus e pera, et pulvis potre in singulos astantes distribuitur, cuius in tubo accensi fumum quisque exugens membra corporis sui singula perflat consecrat-
1050 que. Plura non licuit discere nisi quod videantur notitiam aliquam habuisse diluvii, quo mundus periit propter scelera hominum.

34 · SOLUM

SOLUM

uno mense — 'for one month'
proxima navigatio — 'the next voyage' (of a ship that would carry mail to Europe)
assero, 3 — to claim, declare
fertilis, -e — fertile
solum...fertile — the soil provided sufficient corn and garden vegetables, but proved to be especially good for tobacco, which soon became the main staple of Maryland's farmers.
fraga, -orum —strawberries
vitis, -is, f. — vine
saxifragium, -ii — sassafras
glans, glandis, f. —acorn
iuglans, -ndis, f. walnut
passim — here and there, far and wide, throughout
calco, 1 — to tread on
crassitudo, -inis, f. — thickness, density
insterno, 3 — to spread over
pinguis, -is — rich
rubens, -ntis — red
argilla, -ae — clay
praecelsus, -a, -um — very high
fons, -fontis, m. — spring
potus, -us, m. — drink
subministro, 1 — to supply
cervus, -i — deer

1055 Uno tantum mense hic fuimus, itaque cetera proximae navigationi servanda sunt. Illud assero, solum videri in primis fertile; fraga, vites, saxifragium, glandes, iuglandes, passim
1060 densissimis in silvis calcamus. Nigra et mollis terra unius pedis crassitudine insternitur pingui et rubenti argillae. Praecelsae ubique arbores, nisi ubi a paucis cultus ager. Copia fontium
1065 potum subministrat. Animalia nulla apparent praeter cervos, castorem et sciuros, qui lepores Europaeos adaequant. Infinita vis avium est versicolorum ut aquilarum, ardearum,
1070 cygnorum, anserum, perdicum, anatum. Ex quibus coniectura est non deesse regioni quae vel commodis vel voluptati habitantium subserviant.

1056 caetera *ms* 1057 Solum *in marg. sin.*
1073 42 *altera manus addidit ad dextram in marg. inferiore*

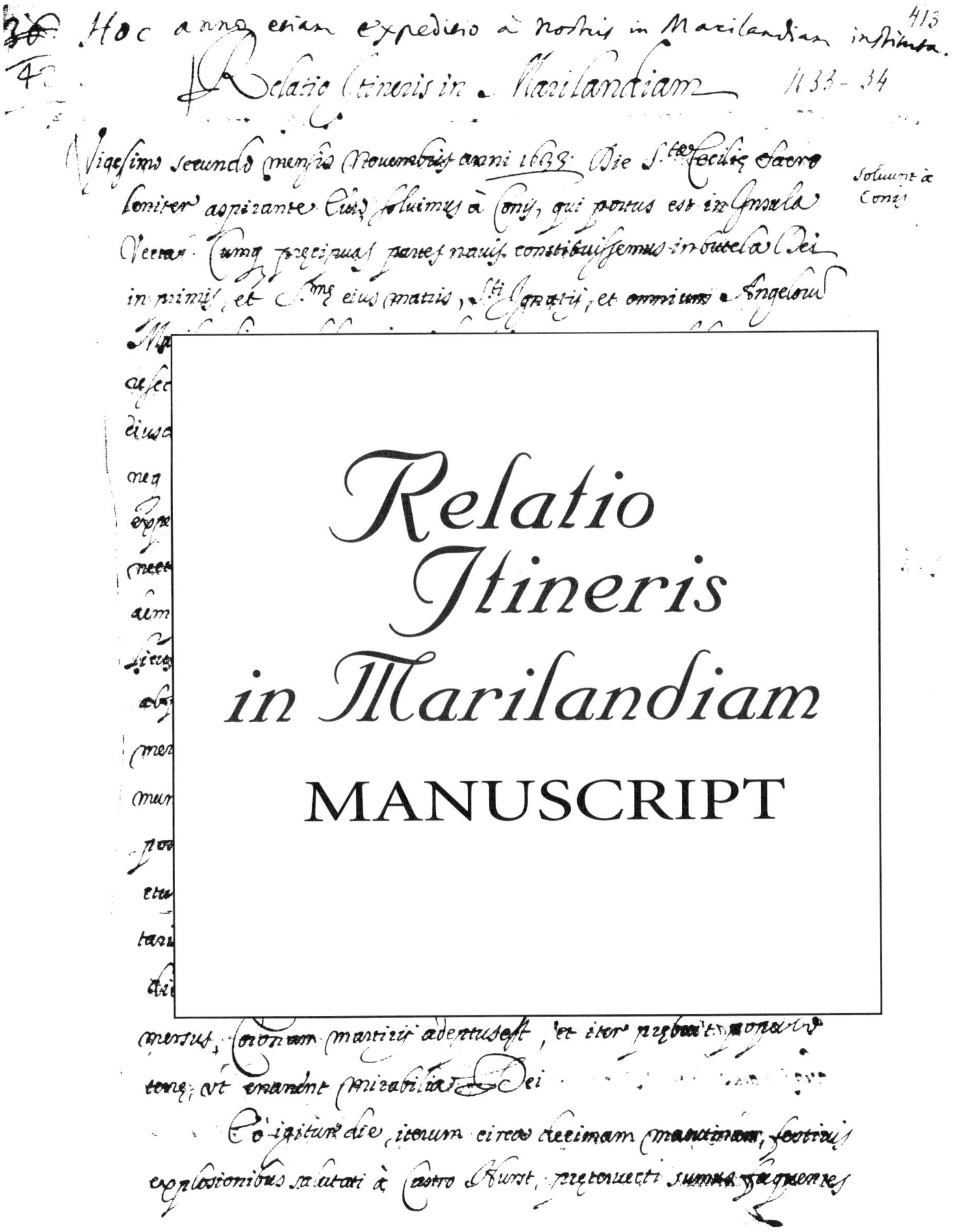

30. 4. Hoc anno etiam expeditio à nostris in Marilandiam instituta. 413

Relatio Itineris in Marilandiam 1133-34

Vigesimo secundo mensis Novembris anni 1633. Die S.tae Caeciliae sacro leniter aspirante Euro, solvimus à Cowes, qui portus est in Insula Vecta. Cumque praecipuas partes navis constituissemus in tutela Dei in primis, et S.mae eius matris, S.ti Ignatii, et omnium Angelorum Solvunt à Cowes

…

mersus, coronam martirii adeptus est, et iter praebuit … tone, ut enarrent mirabilia Dei

Eo igitur die, iterum circa decimam matutinam, festivis explosionibus salutati à Castro Hurst, praetervecti sumus sequentes

Relatio Itineris in Marilandiam

MANUSCRIPT

20 Hoc anno etiam expeditio à nobis in Mailandiam instituta.   413

4   Relatio Itineris in Mailandiam   1133 - 34

Vigesimo secundo mensis Novembris anni 1633. Die S.te Cæciliæ sacro   Solvimus à
leniter aspirante Euro, solvimus à Cony, qui portus est in Insula   Cony
Vectis. Cumque præcipuas partes navis constituissemus in tutela Dei
in primis, et Smæ eius matris, Sti Ignatij, et omnium Angelorum
Mailandiæ, paululum inter duas horas movetur, deficiente vento
recessimus è Regione Castri Yarmouth, quod est ad occasum æstivum
eiusdem Insulæ. Die festis tormentorum tonitruis exceptus sumus,
neque tamen ab metu aberat. Naues enim inter se mussitabant
expectare se Londino Nuntium, et Litteras, atque ideo moras etiam
necessarias videbantur: Sed Deus consilia adversa accepit: Eadem quippe nocte, missuro, sed valido flante vento, Lembus Sal-
ticus (qui eodem portu nobiscum constiterat) solvere coactus, prope
abfuit in nostram Celocem pro impingeret: Illa igitur, ne præci-
meretur, una præcisa, ac deperditis ancora, vela dare quammini-
mum, et quoniam eo loci fluctuans periculosum erat, in mare
potius se demittere festinat, Itaque ne Celocis nostræ conspectum perderemus, sequi decrevimus: Ita quæ Naues in nos agitarunt consilia sunt disturbata. Accidit id præ. Novembris,
die Sto Clementi Sacro, qui anchoræ alligatus, et in mare
mersus, coronam martirii adeptus est, et iter præbuit nonnullis
tenere, ut emanent mirabilia Dei.

        Eo igitur die, iterum circa decimam matutinam, festivis
explosionibus salutati à Castro Hurst, prætervecti summa sequentes

Acus

Acus

scopulos ad extremum Insulae nectit, quos à forma Acus vocant: Cum
autem navigantibus Venoni propter duplicem æstum maris, hinc in scapha
illinc in vicinum illud accipientem, et allidentem naues, ut alte-
rium interim discrimen vaream, quo defuncti sumus ad Castra varie-
mouet; Nam vento, et æstu vrgente, cum nonnrum peccatarantur
eluctationes, prope erat, vt nauis ad terram allideretur, nisi
subito vi magna auersi; eam mari immergente, periculum Deo
propitio elusissemus, qui hoc etiam maiorem Protectionis suæ nos
dignatus est munire sui Clementis.

Die illo, qui in Sabbatum incidit, et nocte insequenti, uentis vt sumus ita Secundis vt postera die mane circa totam,
noctem aliquoties à tergo Promontorium, Snottæ occiduum, et
Insulas Sillinas, placido cursu maris in Occasum uersi, legentes
Oceanum Britannicum, neque quantum potuissemus accelerantes, ne Celocem nius nimis requirente, illa scarci et Gu-
natis maverillas plurimum infestantibus, rheda fieret.

Hinc factum est, vt oneraria insignis vasorum
sexcentorum, cui nomen à Dracone datum est, eam con-
trario profecta Angliam peteret, nos circa tertiam meri-
dianam assequeretur. Et quoniam periculo defuncti turba-
tis iam aliquid admittere vacabat, iucundum erat spectare
duas naues inter se cursu et velarum comparatione inter a
contendentes, eas, et ventis arridentibus. Et viceralis nostra quamuis sinaro non vincemur, misi silentium

415

fuisset ...r Celocem, quæ bardior erat; itaque cessimus one-
rariæ, illa autem ante uesperam præteruecta, conspectui nostro
se subduxit.

Iactabi-i
tempestate

Die igitur Dominica 24. et die Lunæ, et 25. No-
uembris usque ad uesperam prospera usi sumus nauigatione;
Cum uerò uentis in Aquilonem conuersis tanta exorta est
tempestas, ut onerarioa, quam dixi Londinensis retrobracto
cursu, Angliam, et portum apud Paumonios celebrem repetierit. Celox etiam nostra uasorum tantum 40. cum esset,
uiribus cæpit diffidens, et adnauigans monuit se, si naufragium metueret, id luminibus è carchesio ostensis significaturam.
Vehebamur interim nos ualida naui uasorum quadringentorum,
neque aptior ex ligno, et ære construi poterat. Nauareti
uehebamur peritissimo, data est itaque illi optio redeundi si
uellet in Angliam, uel cum uentis porro colluctandi, quibus
si cederet, expectabat nos è proxima littus Hybernicum cæcis
scopulis, et frequentissimis naufragiis infame. Vicit
tamen Nauarchi audax animus, et desiderium probandi,
quæ uires essent nouæ, quam tum primum tractabat, naui.
Sedit animo experiri mare, quod eo fatebatur esse periculo-
sius, quo angustius.

Neque periculum longe aberat, uentis enim ingenti-
bus, et mari exasperato circa mediam noctem uidere erat

Celox perdita

Celocem procul duo lumina e Carelesis proiicientem ... scilicet actum de illa esse, et aliis caustam ueritius existimabamus
momento enim conspectum effugerat, neq. nisi post sex septimanas
eius inditium aliquod ad nos emanauit. Itaque periisse Celoce
cunctis erat persuasum; meliora tamen prouiderat Deus; nam
se fluctibus imparem sentiens mature. Oceanum Virginium
eum quo iam nos luctabamur, deuitans, in Angliam ad
Insulas Sillinas reuertit; unde post liminis Dracone
comite ad Sinum magnum, nos ad Insulas Antillas, ut
dicemus, est assecuta, Deo cui minimorum cura est, et qui
nauicule et Duce, et Custode respiciente.

nauis fluuiis
amissa

At uero nos euentus ignaros dolor, et metus urgeme-
bat, quem tetra nox frequentibus foeda terroribus augebat
illucescente die, cum Africum haberemus contrarium, quia
tamen languidior erat, per multas ambages lente mouebe-
bamur, Ita martis, mercurii, et Iouis dies uariantibus
uentis exiguo profectu abiere. Die Veneris obtinente
humoro, et glaucas cogente nubes uento grauidas, tam ... circa
uesperam se turbo effudit, ut momentis singulis inuoluen-
di fluctibus uideremur. Neque mitiora promittebat dies insequens Andreae Apostoli sacra. Nubes terrificum in morem in dies concrescentes remori erant intuentibus, antequam
discinderentur, et opinionem faciebant adortos aduersum nos

417

in aciem omnes Spiritus tempestatum maleficas, et malos genios
omnes. Marilandiæ Inclinante die uidit Nauarchus Pisces
Solis cursui Solari obnitentem, quod eouidem tempestatis certis=
simum inditium; neque fides abfuit auguris. Item circa de=
cimam nocturnam eaca nubes atrocem depluit imbrem. Nunc
tam immanis turbo Suscepit, ut necesse fuerit quantocyus ad
uela contrahenda accurrere, neque id fieri tam expedite potuit,
quam Acatium, seu uelum maius, quo solo nauigabamus, medio
à Summo deorsum finderetur. Eius pars una in mare dela=
ta, agrè recepta est.

Hic fortissimi cuiusq siue uectoris, siue nautæ esto
consternabus animus, fatebantur enim uidisse se celsas naues
minori procella præcipitatas. Accendit uerò is turbo Catholi=
corum preces, et uota in honorem B.mæ Virginis matris, et
Immaculatæ eiusdem Conceptionis, S.ti Ignatij Patroni
Marilandiæ; S.ti Michaelis, et Aurelariorum omnium ibidem
Angelorum. Et quisque animum suum Sacræ exomolo=
gesi expiare contendebat; nam claui moderamine amisso,
nauigium iam undis, et uentis derelictam fluctuabat, ut in
aqua discas, dum Deus saluti uiam aperiret. Initio fateor
occupauerat me metus amittendæ nauis, et uitæ; postea uero
quam tempus aliquod orationi minus pro more meo quoti=
diano tepide impendissem, atque Christo Domino, B.mæ

Piscis
Solis

Vota, et
preces Ca=
tholicorum

Virgini, Sto Ignatio, et Angelis Marilandiæ exposuissem,
propositum huius itineris esse, Sanguinem Redemptoris nostri
in salutem Barbarorum honorare, eidem servatori Ægram (si
conatus totius secundos dignetur) erigere, florem a veram
Immaculatæ Virgini Matri consecrare, et similia multa, affulsit meas in animis consolatio non mediocris, et simul persuasio tam certa, nos non ab hac procella tantum, sed ab
omni alia, itinere isto, liberandos, ut nullus apud me esse
posset dubitandi locus: Dederam me orationi, cum mare
sæviret, maxime (et quod ad Dei unius gloriam cedat)
vix dum eam finieram, cum cæpisse animadverte tam
tempestatem, Id scilicet me nova quadam me induit habitu
animi, perfuditq simul gaudio ingenti, et admiratione
cum propensam Dei in Marilandiæ populos voluntatem
(ad quos R. V. nos misit) haud paulo amplius persentirem. Dulcissima Redemptoris nostri bonitas in æternum
laudetur. Amen.

Cum itaque deferbuisset iam mare, reliqua trium mensium
navigatio placidissima fuit, ut Navarchus cum suis, iucundiorem se vidisse nunquam, aut quietiorem asseveraverit, neque enim unius horæ passi sumus incommodum. Cum vero
tres menses nominis, non dies, nos tamdiu mare insequ[...]tes,
sed iter integrum, et mare, quas in Americ[...] [...]

Perdelita
Salus

adnumero; Nauigatio enim ipsa septem hebdomadas, et duos
solummodo dies tenuit, idq̃ censetur iter expeditum.

Ab eo igitur tempore quando littus Hispaniæ legebamus, ⟨A Suriis
neque aduerso, neque uento admodum prospero vsi sumus q̃   necuunt⟩
uerebamur Suereas, nullos tamen habuimus obuios, receperat
fortasse se ad solemne ieiunium, quod eam, som uocant, celebrandum, in illam enim anni tempestatem incidebat; præ-
teruectis autem fretum Herculeum, et Maderas, et ventis
puppi uela implentibus (qui non iam uagi, sed ad Austral
et Africum, qui noster erat cursus, constanter sedens)
apparuerunt tres naues, quarum vna nostram mole supera-
uat, distare autem uidebantur ad tres circiter Leucas versus
Occidentem, et nobis obuiam conari, interdum etiam ad
inuicem ultro, citroq̃ mittere, et percontari. Cum suspicaremur esse Sureanum Pyraticas, expediebamus quæcumque
ad pugnam erant necessaria. Neque deerant ex nostris
qui Nauarchum imprudentius stimularent, vt eas vltro aggrederetur, ac lacesseret; sed Dominum habebat, cui cum reddenda erat ratio, probabilem se posse pugnæ causam afferre dubitabat; Et quidem conflictum difficilem habiturum
fuisse existimo : quamquam fortasse quantum ab illis
nos, tantum nos illi pertimebant, et erant, vt coniectura
assequor mercatores, qui ad fortunatas, non procul

diffitas tendebant, et uel non poterant nos assequi, uel
nolebant.

Hinc ad Insulas fortunatas delati, Sinu magno
suscepti fuimus, in quo nullus metus, nisi à Malaciis, quæ
cum 15. diebus, et tribus aliquando septimanis perdurant
deficit nauigantes commeatus. Id uero raro; et uix seculo
uno semel, aut iterum accidit: frequentissimè nihilominus
trahendæ sunt moræ, deficiente uento, qui cum spirat, unus
et idem semper est cui nostræ nauigationi proficuus. In
hoc Sinu confecimus milliarium Gallicorum bis mille, pleno
passu uelis mare secantes; lacteum, nusquam impedientes malacia, nisi quandoq circa meridiem una hora.

Haud facilem inuenio rationem, tam constantis uenti,
nisi forte id oriri quis dixerit ex uicinia solis inter duos
Tropicos intercurrentis, et ui sua attrahentis ex mari duo
genera meteorum, siccum unum ex marina salsedine, alterum humidum ratione aquæ, ex priori fit uentus; ex posteriori generantur pluuiæ, solitaque utrumque ad se
euehendi causa est, cur eundem cum Sole obliquum semper
cursum seruent, Solemq perpetuò sequantur: Atq eadem
potuit esse ratio, cur inter duos Tropicos ex rerum summus,
ingentem simul calorem, et copiosam pluuiam ideo constanter
mane, meridie, uespere, uel saltem uentos in locis uehementiores

421

Hinc etiam deduci potest ratio, cur hoc tempore sinus à malacijs liber fuerit. Nam Sol in Tropico Capricorni existens, ultra lineam æquinoctialem, et ad eiusdem lineæ extremam partem meridionalem declinans (ut nobis accidit inter 19.ᵐ et 17.ᵐ gradum æquatoris positis) quando mensibus nostris hybernis calores sunt ibi, quanti æstiui (mensibus in Europa) attrahit oblique uentum, et pluuiam ad lineam æquinoctialem, atque inde ijs mensibus uenti sunt certiores, et in hoc Sinu præsertim, et uersus Tropicum Cancri frequentiores, autem sunt malaciæ, cum æstiuo tempore sol æquatorem transit ad nos, attrahito maricas salsas, et aqueas non oblique, sed ferè perpendiculariter.

Hic autem nonpossum non extollere diuinam bonitatem, quæ diligentibus Deum facit, ut omnia cooperentur in bonum. Si enim nulla iniecta mora licuisset eo tempore soluere quo constitueramus, mensis scilicet Augusti uigesimo, Sole eis æquatorem uerticem feriente, intensissimi calores non solum Annonæ labem, sed plerisq' omnibus morbos, mortemq' attulissent. Mora salubi fuit, nam hyeme conscendentes huiusmodi incommodis caruimus, et si consuetas nauigantibus nauseas expirias, nemo morbo aliquo correptus est usque ad festum Natiuitatis Domini. Is dies, ut celebrior esset propinatum est uinum, quo qui usi sunt

Morbi ex Vino

Intemperantius, febri correpti sunt proxima luce numero triginta; Et ex iis non ita multo post, morbui sunt circiter duodecim, inter quos duo Catholici, magnum sui apud omnes desiderium reliquerunt Nicolaus Fairfaxius, et Jacobus Barefote.

^ post conspectum piscem solis qui circa solis obitium, eo est index tempestatum, post tempestatem non unam,

Pisces volantes

Inter navigandum multa, occurrebant curiosa, in primis Pisces ^volantes, qui modo æquor, modo aëra sublime pennis secabant, passerum magnitudine, vel maiorum seu anatular, quas valde etiam gustu pergrato referunt. Centeni gregatim se in aëra librant Delphinos cum fugiunt insequentes. Saub aliqui deficiente pinnarum remigii in nostram navem deciderunt; nam uno impetu non amplius, quam ducros, vel trium iugerum spatium pervolant, cum pinnas acres verberando exsiccatas aquis cursus immergunt, et se iterum fugæ committunt. Cum ab æquatore vno, et viginti gradibus, et aliquot minutis abessemus, vbi Tropicus incipit

Aves Tropicæ

videre erat Aves, quas à loco Tropicas vocant in aëre pendulas; illæ cum falconem mole, adæquent, duabus vng longis, et albentibus, plumis in caudas conspicuæ, incertum est an aëri perpetuo insideant, an quandoo aquis se fuscirent. Cætera ut aliorum litteris nota omitto.

Cum Insulas fortunatas essemus ingenuedi Comes Leonardus Caluert Præfectus Claris agitare cæpit, qua...
mercs

423

merces, et unde comparari posset naui adduci onerandæ, quo
fratris sui Baronis de Baltimor sumptibus caueret; illi
enim (ut totius nauigationis Principi) onus integrum incumbebat. In Virginia à nostratibus nihil commodi sperabatur,
sunt enim huic nouæ plantationi infensi. Itaque ad Insulam
Sti Christophori tendebamus, cum consilio ad libito, ueritiq; ne
ea anni serà tempestate, alij nos præuenissent, prora obuer-
timus ad Austrum, ut Bonauistæ potiremur: quæ Insula
Angolæ opposita in littore Africano, gradibus 14 ad Æquatore, Statio est Holandorum Salem conquirentium, quem
deinde uel domum, uel ad piscem in Groelandia condiendum
conferunt. Copia Salis, atque etiam caprarum, quarum Insula
ferax est eò nos inuitabat: nam alioqui habitatore nullo
utitur: Pauci tantum Lusitani ex ilio propter scelera
pulsi, vitam, ut possunt, trahunt, uix ducenta milliaria
confeceramus; cum mutatis iterum quorundam suggestione
consilijs, ne commeatus in tanto circuitu nos deficeret,
deflectimus ad Barbados.

    Est ea Carebum, seu Antillarum Insularum infima,
ab Æquatore 13 tantùm gradibus distans, cæterarumq;
(quæ in modum arcus ad usq; Sinum Mexicanum longo tractu protenduntur) grananium. Ad Eane (ut

[margin note:] Bonauista
Sale et Capris
abundat.

[margin note:] Barbados

appulimus tertio Januarij, in spem venimus mutuarum commoditatum ab Incolis Anglis, et consanguineo Gubernatore; sed conspiratione facta, modium tritici, qui in Insula medio floreno Belgico veniebat, nobis non nisi quintupla proportione duobus florenis cum dimidio vendere decreverunt. Refrendem utrum quinquaginta florenis licitabant. Pullum Indicum viginti quinque, ceteraque gentis utensilia minora tribus florenis, Bovinam, seu verve mananujam exhabant: Vivunt enim rane Indico, et patatis, quod radicum genus tanta affluentia provenit ut plaustra integra gratis aufferre liceat

Divina Provid. Hominum acerbam feritatem Divinae providentiae considerabis mitigavit. Intelleximus enim ad Insulam Bonavijste stare classem Hispanicum, quo expressi omni Salis commercio prohiberent: illo si penes contendissemus itinere constituto, in capes prædæ facti dereliscemur si maiori interim periculo ad Barbados menti, famuli per totam Insulam in necem Dominorum conspirarant; tum scilicet In libertatem asserti, navique nomina appellenet, potiri statuerunt, et tentans maria, coniuratione patefacta per quendam, quem facti atrocitas deterrerat, Supplicium unius ex precipuis, et consciis, crudelitati, et nobis

Salues fuit: nostra enim nauis, ut quæ prima littori applicuit, nisiq, destinata fuerat, et eo ipso die, quo appulimus
octingentos in armis reperimus, quo recentissimo sceleri ob-
uiarent.

Insula Barbadorum

FF: B. Arianda quædam manare ict, quæ ex Insula per-   *Calores immensi*
sex triginta milliaria continet Longitudo, Latitudo 15.
gradibus, 13. distat ab Æquatore, calore tanto, ut Libernis
mensibus Incolæ lineis uestiantur, et aquis se sæpius immergant.
Messis tum erat cum appulimus: nisi frequentes uenti aerem
temperarent, impossibilis esset habitatio. Lecti sunt fora-   *lecti*
gula uestis ex gossipio a parte texta, in hac, cum ex- quiescendi tempus, funibus appensa ad duos hincinde pretores
dormiunt: de die iterum quocumq, liber auferunt. Merces præcipuæ sunt, frumentum, et gossipium. Iucundum
est uidere modum, et copiam pendentis ex arbore Gossipij.   *Gossipium*
Arbor ex qua nascitur maior non est Oxyacantho (quam
Vulgus Berberin uocat) quamquam arbori, quam spinæ
similior: hæc nodum fert magnitudine iuglandis, forma
acutiori, qui in quatuor partes dissectus, Gossipium niue
candidius, et pluma mollius, in speciem nucis conuolutum
fundit. Gossipio sese parua semina insident, uria, æqua-
lia, quæ tempore suo collectum, et rota quadam a semine
expeditum condunt in saccos, et asseruunt.

Ingens
Brassica

Brassicæ genus admirandum est, quæ cum caulem habeat in cubitos, et octoginta pedum altitudinem excrescentes, vel cruda editur, vel elixa caulis ipse ad unius ulnæ mensuram sub fructu habetur in delicijs, crudus admixto pipere saporem Hispanicum superat, et iuglandi nudatæ proprio. Ingens caulis arbori bene magnæ truncum adæquans, neque tamen arbor, sed legumen, brassicam fert non amplius pro Hisdem vidcre est arborem satis proceram, quam Saponem vocant: Grana saponi nucem avellanam non excedunt magnitudine, eorum pinguis tunica, Saponis instar, purgat, et detergit, quamquam, ut aiant, lino benuior inimica. Ex eis granis multas mecum ablatas in Marilandiam, mandavi tenere futurarum arborum semina.

Palma
Cristi

Inter arbores etiam numerant Palmam Cristi, quamquam truncum illa habeat porosum, et leguminissimilem, racemum fere ingentem seminum coloris subcinericij spinis armatam, et nigris maculis inspersum. Ex eis præstans oleum exprimibur. Mala aurea, citrina, granata nuces etiam, quas Hispani cocos vocant, cæteriq, calidar Regionum fructus ubertim proveniunt.

Gnauar

Pupaes

Est, et fructus, qui Gnauar dicibur coloris aurei formæ citri minoris, gustu tamen referens Cydonium. Pupaes coloris est, et formæ non absimili, sed maculis cum sit,

427

conciliandus tantum cibis adhibetur.

Præcellit autem cæteros, quos alibi terrarum gustaui
fructus nuc Pinea. Est ea coloris aurei, viroreq mixta
gratissima, tres, uel quatuor eiusdem nominis nuces Europęas
mole adęquans, figura non admodum dissimili, sed operosiore, non tot distincta oculamentis, et modulis, qui ad
iquem adhibiti nucleum reddant, sed mollis, et tenella inuolu-
ta membranula, gustui iucundissima, nullo aspera acino,
sed a summo deorsum æqualiter palato amidens, neque deest
quam meretur, corona, haud dubiæ enim Regina fructuum
appellari potest. Gustum habet aromaticum, et quantum coniectura assequor, fraga, uina, saccaroq mista referendum.
Sanitati conseruandæ plurimum confert, ea porum confi-
tutioni tam apte consentiens, ut licet ferum expetat, comitem
tamen, si qua us alia, quam maxime corroboret, neque erecta
hanc queras in arbore, sed unam una ex radice, quasi cardu
Hispanici prominentem. Optabam me nucem unam Paternitati Vestrę cum hisce Litteris tradere potuisse in
manus, nihil enim illam præter ipsam pro dignitate potes
describere.

Vigesimo quarto Ianuarij de nocte subductis anchoris, Sta Lucia
et circa meridiem sequentis diei, relicta ad leuem Insula
Stę Lucię, sub Vesperam tenuimus Matelinam. Hic dus Matalina

14
38

In insulis Antillæ sive Carebum reperti obvij

Indios nudorum hominum, molem nostræ navis veniri, Pepones,
Cucurbitas, fructus Platani, et Psittacos, de longe ostentabant
commutandos: Gens effera, procera, obesa, pigmento purpureo
nitens, ignara Numinis, carnium humanarum avida, et quæ
Anglorum interpretes aliquot pridem absumpserat. Regionem
incolit inprimis fertilem, sed quæ tota sylvæ sit, nulla planitie
pervia. A plaustro albo, in signum pacis proposito, eos qui se a
longe ostentabant, invitavimus ad commercia, sed indicium
amoris, insignia conspue... proposuerunt. Cum eis ostensis
quantum æstimus intellexissent, animis resumptis accessere propius, sed tanium tintinnabulis, et cutellis accerbis,
navi non nimium fidentes, Celocem adeunt, promittentes se, si subsisteres decerneremus, sequenti die melioris
mercis allaturos. Capiet olim aliquem, uti spero, derelicti
hujus populi miseratio. Apud nautas increbuit rumor
(oriens a Gallis quibusdam naufragis) reperiri in hac insula
Animal, cujus fronti lapis inusitati splendoris insidet, carum
vel candelæ ardenti similis. Huic animali Carbunc nomen
indiderunt. Rei fides sit penes auctorem.

Die proxima illucescente aliam Carebum insulam
attigimus, quam asperorum montium similitudo Hispanicæ
Guadalupæ fecit cognomen, estq uti confidas his cutela eius
mæ Virginis matris. Unde Monseratem tenuimus circa
...

429

meridiem, ubi ex Lombo galliæ intelleximus, nondum nos ab
Hispanorum classe tutos esse. Habet Monserrate Incolas
Hybernos pulsos ab Anglis Virginiæ ob fidei catholicæ
professionem. Sumus ad Mævium pestilenti aere, et febribus Infamem. Uno die absumpto iter fecimus ad S.tū Christophori,
ubi decem dies substituimus, à Gubernatore Anglo, et Capitaneis duobus Catholicis amice invitati, me in primis benigne accepit
Coloniæ Galliæ in eadem Insula Præfectus.

    Quæcumque apud Barbados rara visuntur, hic etiam
reperi, et præterea non procul à Præfecti Sede montem sulphureum. Et quod admireris magis, Plantam Virginis sic
dictam, quod minimo digiti contactu confestim marcescat,
et contidat quanquam data mora revivescens iterum
surgat. *Ibidem* Locusta arbor, quam su-
spicio est præbuisse victum S.to Joanni Baptistæ ulmam
adæquat altitudine, apibus tam grata, ut libentissime illic
favos suos implicant, mel, si nomen silvestris demas, neque
colore, neq sapore à purissimo, quod gustavi melle differt:
fructus etiam Locustæ nomen retinens in duriori cortice
fabarum, siliquis pari, medullam continet mollem, sed tenacem,
gustu farinæ similem melle mixtæ; Semina fert grandius cu-
las, quatuor, vel quinque coloris castanei, aliqua
inferenda asportavi.

Maui
S. Xpfori

mons sul-
phureus
Planta
Virgo

Locusta
arbor et fru

Caput Consol.is
in Virginia

Ac tandem hic soluentes, Caput quod vocant Consolationis in Virginiæ tenuimus, prǣ Februarij pleni metu, ne quid mali nobis machinarentur Angli Incolǣ, quibus nostra plantatio imprimis incommodum erat. Literǣ tamen quas à Rege, et à summis Angliæ Quæstore ad earum Regionum Præfectum ferebamus, ualebant ad placandos animos, et eas, quæ nobis porro usui futuræ erant impetrandæ. Sperabat enim Præfectus Virginiæ eac beneuolentiæ erga nos, facilius Regis e fiscis Regis ma---- enim pecuniæ sibi debitǣ recuperationum. Sparsum bantum rumorem nuncia bant ad uenire sex naues, quæ omnia sub Hispanicis potestate redigerent. Indigenas ea propter omnes in armis esse, quod uerum postea experti sumus. Rumor tamen uereor, ab Anglis ortum habuit.

Sinus Chesopeac

Post octo, uel nouem dierum benignam tractationem tertio Martij uela facientes, et in Sinum Chesopeaeæ inuecti, cursum ad Aquilonem deflexinus, ut fluuio Patomeac potiremur. Sinus Chesopeaeæ latus decem leucas placidè inter littora labitur, profundus quatuor, quinque, sex, et septem orygio, piscibus, cum fauet annus scaten, iucunditatem aquæ lapsum uix inuenies. edit tamen fluuio Patomeac cuius nomen à S.to Gregorio Indidimus.

Patomeac
fluuius, siue
S. Gregorij

46.

Iam enim optatâ potiti Regione, Nomina pro re nata distribuebamus. Et quidem Promontorium, quod est ad austrum

431

titulo S.ti Gregorii consecrauimus, e Aquilonare S.ti Michaeli, *Promontorium eiusdem S. Michaelis*

in honorem omnium Angelorum Marilandie indigitantes: Maius *Indigenarum*

iucundiusue flumen aspexi nunquam; Nemesis illis comparatus

vix riuulus videri potest, nullis inficitur paludibus, sed solida

vtrinque terra assurgunt decentes arborum Silue, non clausę ue-

preti, uel subnascentibus sarcubis, sed quasi manu lata consitę

vt libere quadrigam inter medias arbores agitare possis. In ipsis

ostis fluminis armatos indigenas conspeximus. Ea nocte ignes

tota Regione arserunt, et quoniam nunquam illis tam magna

nauis conspecta fuit, nuncii hinc inde missi narrabant, *Indigenarum*

Insulę similem aduentasse tot homines, quot in Siluis arbores. *metus, et*

Processimus tamen ad Insulas. Ardearum, sic dictis ab innumeris *admiratio*

examinibus eiusmodi uolucrum: Primam, quę occurrit S.ti *Insulę*

Clementis nomine appellauimus. Secundam S.tę Catharinę. *Ardearum*

tertiam S.tę Cecilię Descendimus primum ad S.ti Clementis,

ad quam nisi vado non patet accessus propter declive littus.

Hic ancillę, quę ad lauandum descenderunt, inuerso lintre *Lintea*

penè submersę sunt, magna parte mecum etiam linteor *deperdita*

deperdita, iactura in iis partibus non mediocri.

Abundat ęe Insula Cedro, Sassifragis, Eruis, et floribus

ad omnis generis accraria componenda, pauce etiam Syluestri,

quę iuglandem fert predurani, spissi putaminis, nucleo parco,

sed mire grato. Cum tamen quadringentorum tantu iugerum

latitudinis visa est non ampla satis futura sedes novæ plantationi: quæsitus est tamen locus castro ædificando ad prohibendos exteros fluvii commercio, finesque tutandos, is enim erat angustissimus fluminis traiectus.

Anno 1634.

Præmissa

Die Annunciationis S.mæ Virginis Mariæ primam in eae Insula Litavimus: id eae Coeli Regione nunquam antea factum: Sacrificio peracto sublata in humeros ingenti Cruce, quam ex arbore dedolaveramus, ad locum designatum ordine procedentes, Præfecto, et Commissariis, cæterisque Catholicis adiuvantibus, propriumque Christo Servatori eriximas Littaniis Stæ Crucis humiliter flexis genibus, magna animorum commotione recitatis.

Cum præfecta

Cum autem intellexisset Præfectus Imperatori Pascatawaye complures parere Regulos, illum adiit habuit, ut operibus itineris nostri causa, et eius unius conciliata voluntate, faciliorad cæterorum animos paveret Ingressus. Itaque iuncta Celoci nostræ altera, quam in Virginia conduperat, et navi in anchoris relicta ad Ebriam Clementem cursu circumacta ad Australem partem fluminis ejscendit. Tumque Barbaros ad interiora fugisse comperisset, progressus est ad civitatem, quæ a flumine desumpto nomine Pacomeaci etiam dicitur. Hic Regi puero tutor erat Patuus nomine Archihu, qui regni vices in Regno habebat, vir gravis, et prudens. Is

Conantur Rep. Pato: meat:

436

P. P. Altram, qui Comes adibus erat Præfecto (me etenim
etiamnum detinebat ad Farinas) quidam, quiq Interpretem
de Gentilium erroribus explicantes, libenter aures dabat, suos
identidem agnoscens: utq edoctus nos non belli causa, sed benevo-
lentiæ gratia eò appulisse, ut gentem (unde civilibus præceptis
imbueremus, et viam ad coelum aperiremus, simul Regionum longinquarum commoda ijs impartituros, gratos advenisse monstravit.
Interpres erat ex Protestantibus Virginiæ, itaq eum plura pro
tempore disserere non posset Pater, promisit se non ita multo
post reversurum. Id mihi ex animo accidit, inquit Arcadius,
una mensa utemur, mei quoq aspectu pro se renatus ibunt, erunt
inter nos omnia communia.

Hinc itur ad Pascatauuaye, ubi omnes ad arma convo-
Et Imperator larant, Quingenti circiter arcubus Instructi in littore cum
Imperatore constiterant, Signis pacis datis, Imperator ratu posito
Celocem conscendit, et audito nostrorum benevolo erga eas gentes
animo, facultatem dedit, qua Imperij eius parte vellemus habitandi

Interim dum Præfectus apud Imperatricem in itinere
esset Barbari ad S.bus Clementem audentioes facti, se vigilibus
nostris familiarius admiscebant. Excubias enim interdiu, noctuq
agebamus, tum (ut Lignatores nostros, tum ut Agri actum
quem tabulis, costiq solutis allatum ædificabamus, ab repentibus Insol-
tibus tutaremur; Voluntati erat audire admirantes singula. In primis utinam tenere tanta ardor exercuisset, ex quo cum immisi

moles navis dedolaretur, excisam enim arbitrarentur admodum Indicæ Canoæ ex vno aliquo arboris trunco. Frumenta maiora attonitos onere, i tenebant, haud parum quippe vt caetera, erant stridulis ipsorum arcubus, et bombardis ...

Interea Socium itineris ad Imperatorem adtinuerat Henricum Fleet Capitaneum ex iis, qui in Virginia commorantur, domino Baltimore in primis gratum, et ipsius tocouium peritum. Hic initio nobis perfamiliaris, deinde Claborni cuiusdam sinistris seductus consilijs, infensissimus effectus. Indigenarum animos quā ante potest aduersus nos accendit; Interim tamen ... dum inter nos amicum agebat, Sedem Præfecto monstrauit qualem vix Europa meliorem Dei benignitate ostendere potest.

Igitur A Sto Clemente nouem circiter leucas progressi ad Aquilonem, fluminis ostio Appulsi sumus, cui a Sto Georgio nomen indidimus. Id flumen ab Austro ad Aquilonem ad viginti circiter miliaria procurrit antequam salsedine marinæ exuatur, Thamesi non dissimile. In eius ostio duo visuntur sinus 300 nauium immensæ molis capaces. Sinum vnum Sto Georgio conseruauimus, alterum inferius Beatissimæ Virgini Mariæ. Leua pars fluminis Sedes erat Regis yaocomico, nos ad dextram excendimus, et ad milliæ passus à littore auulsi, ciuitati designatæ nomen à Sta Maria posuimus; vtque omnem speciem iniuriæ, inimicitiarumque occasionem præuerteremus, appensis in commutationem

455

securibus, ascijs, castris, et monilibus aliquot panni, emimus à
Rege triginta tere illius milliaria, cui Regioni Augusta Carolina iam nomen est.

Sasquelanoes, gens bellis assueta, Regi yaocomis præ
ceteris infesta, frequentibus incursibus omnem depopulabitur
agrum, et incolas ad alias quærendas Sedes, periculi metu
adigit. Hæc causa est cur tam prompte partem eius Regni
impetrauimus; Deo uiam legi suæ, et Lumini æterno iis
adminiculis aperiente. Migrant alij, atq alij quotidie, nobisq
relinquunt domos, agros, noualia. Id profecto miraculo simile est, homines Barbaros paucis antea diebus in armis
aduersum nos paratos tam faciles se nobis uelut agnos permittere, nobis se, suaq tradere. Digitus Dei est hic, et
magnum aliquod emolumentum huic nationi meditabitur
Deus. Paucis tamen quibusdam permittitur adhuc suo
inter nos habitatio in annum proximum. Sum uero liber
nobis relinquendus est ager.

Indigenæ statura sunt procera, et decenti, cute
à natura subfusca, quam colore plerumq rubeo misto oleo
inficientes, ut culices arceant, tetricam reddunt, commodo
suo magis jntenti, quam decori. Vultum alijs etiam coloribus deturpant à naso sursum carulei, deorsum rubicundi, uel
è contra uarijs, et sane fœdis, terrificisq modis. Et quoniam

Augusta
Carolina

Sasquelanoes

Indigenar
species

barba in ultimam prope aetatem event, atq mentis barba
simulant, lineis uary coloris ac eptimy labii; led aures arrodunt;
Caesariem, quam plerumque nigram nutriunt, in modum ad Sini
stram aurem circumductam uittas astringunt; addita aliquo quod
apud ipsos in pretis sit monili. Quidam in fronte ngferunt
piscis figuram cupream. Colla muniunt uitriis globuli; filis
insertis more torquium; quanquam et globuli uiliores apud
ipsos esse incipiant, et commercio minus futiles.

Variantur ut plurimum pelle ceruina, uel similis
generis pelle, quod a tergo fluit in modum pallii, cincti ad
ad umbilicum perizomatis, caetera nudi. Impubes pueri,
puellaeq nulla re tecti uagantur. Plantis pedum ut et
cornu durius spinas, tribulosq calcant illaesi. Arma sunt
arcus, et sagitta duos cubitos longae, cornu ceruino, uel albo
praeacuto silice armatae, eas tanta arte iaciant, ut passere
eminus medium configant. Utq se ad peritiam expercent
—otum in sublime iaciunt, tum im rursam meno sagittam
intigunt antequam decidat: Arcu eximia non admodum
contento utuntur, metam longe positam serire non possunt:
His armis uiuunt, et quotidie p arcus, et siluas sciuras
perdices, pullos gallicos, seica uenantur: Horum enim
omnium ingens est copia, quamquam nondum nobis
ipsis expeditus alimentis praematu aureamuy meta insiciuiust.

437

Domos habitant ouali forma oblonga constructas
nouem, uel decem pedes albas. In eas lumen à tecto admit- *Domus*
titur fenestra cubitali, illa fumo etiam auferendo inseruit;
nam ignem medio in pauimento accendunt, et circa ignem
dormiunt. Reges tamen, et Principes uiri sua habeant
uelut conclauia, et lectum quatuor fulcris in terram adactis,
et asseribus superpositis instratum; ~~mihi, et sociis~~ ex iis
casulis una obrigit, in qua sal pro tempore commodè
habentur, donec edificia parentur laxiora. Quam primum
Marilandiæ Sacellum dixeris quanquam eadi paulo
decentius instructum, quam cum ab Indis habitabatur.
Proxima nauigatione, si Deus captis annuat, non
deerunt nostris, quæ cæteris in domibus sunt usui
necessaria.

    Gentis Indoles ingenua est, et lata, et quæ *Indoles*
probe capiat cum proponitur, gustu excellunt, et odoratu *Victus*
uix etiam Europeos superant. Victitant plerumque
pulte, quem Pone, et Omini appellant, utraq ex
tritico conficitur, adduntq interdum piscem, ad quod
uenatu, aucupioq assecuti sunt. Cauent sibi quam maxi-
mè à uino, et potionibus calidis, ~~quæ~~ adducuntur
facile, ut eas dejurent, nisi quos Angli suis uitiis
infererint. Quod ad castitatem attinet, fateor me

pondum aduertisse in uiro, uel femina actionem ullam,
quæ uel leuitatem saperet, quotidie tamen nobiscum, et
apud nos sunt, et nostris quidem ubi consortio, occurrunt
sponte; uultu ad hilaritatem composito, et offerunt
quæ uenati, uel piscati fuerint, libros etiam aliquando
et ostrea cocta uel assa, idq́ paucis inuitati lingua
ipsis uernacula, uerbis, quæ per signa hactenus utcumque didicimus. Plures ducunt uxores, integram
tamen seruant fidem coniugalem. Mulierum aspectus
grauis est, et modestus. In uniuersum liberales nutriunt animos, quicquid beneficij contuleris, rependunt.
Nil temere decernunt, aut subito amenti motu arripiunt
sed ratione; ideo cum quidquam momenti aliquando
proponitur; silent aliquandiu cogitabundi, tum aiunt
breuiter, aut negant, et propositi sunt tenacissimi.
Hi profecto si semel Christianis præceptis imbuantur
(et quidem nihil obstat uidetur præter linguæ his regionibus usitatæ defectum) uirtutis, humanitatis q́ cultores
egregij euadent: miro tenentur desiderio ciuilis conuersatio-
nis, Europaeorum q́ indumentorum. Iamq́ iisdem usti-
bus fuissent usi, ni auaritia mercatorum obstitisset, qui
pannos nisi Castore non commutant. Castorem uero uniuscuiusq́
uenari non potest. Absit, ut eorum auaritia eo usque imitemur

439

Religio

Idiomatis ignaris, facit ut quid novus de Religione
sentiant, nondum constet. Interpretibus enim protestantibus
minus fidimus: Ex pauca raptim didicimus. Unum Deũ
cœli agnoscunt, quem Deum nostrum vocant; nullum tamen
honorem externum illi exhibent: omni verò ratione placare conantur: planat eum quendam spiritum, quem Otke
nominant, ut ne noceat: frumentum, ut aluis, et ignem
colunt, ut Deos humani generis mirè beneficos. Hanc ceremoniam quidam è nostris in templo Bareluxem vidisse se
narrant. — Die constituto è pluribus pagis convenere,
circa ingentem ignem omnes omnium ætatum: viri, fœminæq
proximè ad ignem stabant, iuniores, pone illos reve-
rentiori: Dum adipe cervino in ignem coniecta, et sublatis
in cœlum manibus, et vocibus clamabant omnes Sako Sako.
Intervallo facto profert unus aliquis benè m ignem peram.
In pera est tubus, et puluis, quem Potee nominant. Tubus
est quali nostrates vtuntur ad expugendum fumum tabacci, sed multo maior: Igitur pera circa ignem ferbur
sequentibus pueris, et puellis, et vocer satis gratas alternantibus Sako Sako. Circulo peracto eximitur tubus è pera,
et puluis Potee in singulos astantes distribuitur, cuius
in tubo accensi fumum quisq expirens membra corporis
sui singula perflat, consecratq. Plura non licuit discere

nisi quod videantur novitias aliquam habuisse diluuij
quo mundus periijt propter scelera hominum.

Vno tantum mense hic fuimus, itaq̃ cetera
proxima nauigationi seruanda sunt. Illa vero, solum
ardent in primis fertile, fragrant vites, sapi magium glanz
des iuglandes, panem densissimis In filuis calcamus;
Nigra, et mollis terra vnius pedis crassitudines insternitur
pingui, et rubenti argille, precelss vbiq̃ arbores, nisi vbi
a paucis cultus ager. Copia fontium rerum subministrat.
Animalia nulla aparent, preter Ceruos, Castorem, et
Sciuros, qui lepores Europeos adequant. Infinita
est auium vel vorticulorum, vt Aquilarum, Ardearum
Cygnorum, Anserum, Perdicum Anatum. Dẽ quibus
coniectura rest, non deesse Regioni, que vel commodis,
vel voluptati habitantium subseruiant.

ILLUSTRATIONS

Special thanks to Jeff D. Goldman,
Photo Services, Maryland Historical Society.

INDEX

	DATE DUE		